The Shrinking Library Dollar

Dantia Quirk
and
Patricia Whitestone

Knowledge Industry Publications, Inc.
White Plains, NY and London

Communications Library

The Shrinking Library Dollar

Library of Congress Cataloging in Publication Data

Quirk, Dantia.
The shrinking library dollar.

(Communications Library)
Includes index.
1. Libraries and publishing—United States.
2. Book industries and trade—United States.
3. Library finance—United States. I. Whitestone, Patricia. II. Title. III. Series.
Z716.6.Q575   025.1'1'0973   81-12319
ISBN 0-914236-74-1   AACR2

Acknowledgement

    Knowledge Industry Publications, Inc. wishes to thank the many firms and individuals who cooperated with the gathering of data for this work and its earlier edition, an industry study entitled *The Library Market for Publications and Systems,* published in 1978. In particular, we wish to single out the Book Industry Study Group. This not-for-profit corporation, funded by organizations concerned with the future of the book industry, has contributed significantly to an understanding of book publishing by its research efforts. This book has been aided immeasurably by its findings. All tables cited as derived from its publications are © 1980 by the Book Industry Study Group and are reprinted with permission. We also wish to thank the Association of American Publishers and Association of Media Producers for use of statistics gathered by those organizations, which are © 1979 and © 1980 by AAP and AMP respectively, and are reprinted with permission.

Printed in the United States of America

Copyright ©1982 by Knowledge Industry Publications, Inc., 701 Westchester Ave., White Plains, NY 10604. Not to be reproduced in any form whatever without written permission from the publisher.

Table of Contents

List of Tables ii

1. Introduction 1

2. Overview of Libraries in the U.S. 9

3. The Library Market for General Books 46

4. The Library Market for Professional and Reference Books 62

5. The Library Market for Periodicals 75

6. The Library Market for Systems 92

7. The Library Market for Audiovisual and Other Materials 111

8. Summary and Conclusions 126

Profiles 142

Selected References 165

Index 167

About the Authors 170

List of Tables

1.1: Libraries and Library Budgets in the United States, 1980 2
1.2: Library Budgets and Estimated Acquisitions of Publications, Systems and Supplies, 1980 3
1.3: Book Industry Study Group Estimates of Materials Acquisitions by All Libraries, 1980 4

2.1: Estimated Number of Librarians by Type of Library, 1960 and 1970; Projected Requirements, 1980 and 1990 12
2.2: Percent of Funds and Expenditures from Various Sources for Public Libraries in Smallest and Largest Cities 14
2.3: Estimated Public Library Materials Acquisitions, Even Years, 1976-1984..16
2.4: Rank Order of Public Libraries With 1 Million or More Volumes in their Collections: United States, 1974 & 1978 18
2.5: Expenditures of 10 Large Public Libraries, 1977-1981 20
2.6: Public Library Collections, 1962 and 1974 22
2.7: Public Library Operating Expenditures, 1962 and 1974 23
2.8: Selected Statistics on Collections, Staff and Operating Expenditures of the 10 Largest Academic Libraries, 1976-77 ..24
2.9: Leading Academic Libaries Ranked by Expenditures for Materials, 1976-77 25
2.10: General Statistics of College and University Libraries, Outlying Areas, 1970-71, 1975-76 and 1976-77 28
2.11: Academic Library Statistics, 1973-74, 1976-77 and 1979-80......30
2.12: Estimated Academic Library Materials Expenditures, Even Years, 1976-1984..31
2.13: Operating Expenditures of Academic Libraries, 1963 and 1975 ..31
2.14: Expenditures for Public School Libraries by Purpose and Level of School, 1974 and 1978 32
2.15: School Library/Media Center Collections and Acquisitions, 1974 33
2.16: Estimates of School Library Acquisitions, Even Years, 1976-1984..35
2.17: Estimates of Special Library Acquisitions, Even Years, 1976-1984..35
2.18: Statistics of Federal Libraries, FY 1972 and FY 1978 37
2.19: Percentage Distribution of Expenditures for Public Libraries and Public Schools, 1972, 1974 and 1975 39

2.20:	General State and Local Government Expenditures for Selected Areas, 1972-73, 1975-76 and 1978-79	40
2.21:	Federal Funding for Major Library Programs, Fiscal Years 1977-1981	42
3.1:	Estimated Acquisitions by U.S. Libraries of Domestic Trade Books, 1978-1984	47
3.2:	Book Publishing Costs at Alternative Levels of Production	49
3.3:	Profit and Loss Statement for a Trade Book Selling 40,000 Copies	50
3.4:	Leading Hardcover Publishers Based on 1979 Sales	50
3.5:	List Prices of Selected Hardcover Fiction and Nonfiction Trade Books, 1980	53
3.6:	Book Review Media, 1977 and 1979	56
3.7:	Domestic Net Trade Book Sales by Type of Customer, 1979	58
3.8:	Leading Book Wholesalers, 1980	59
4.1:	Estimated Acquisitions Expenditures by U.S. Libraries for Domestically Published Professional and Reference Books, 1978-1984	63
4.2:	Sales of Professional Books, 1979	65
5.1:	Estimated Library Market for Periodicals, Even Years, 1976-1984	76
5.2:	Periodical Publishing Revenue and Percentage from Advertising and Circulation, 1975-1981	78
5.3:	Leading Mass Circulation Magazines of Interest to Libraries, 1980	81
5.4:	Leading Special Interest Magazines of Importance to Libraries, 1980	81
5.5:	Scholarly and Research Journals, 1977	82
5.6:	Leading Publishers of Scholarly and Research Journals	83
5.7:	Circulation Categories of Scholarly and Research Journals	85
5.8:	Average Increase in Journal Circulation by Category, 1972-1977	85
5.9:	Comparison of Journal Prices, 1978-80	86
5.10:	Number of Periodicals Held by Academic Libraries	87

6.1:	Major U.S. Online Bibliographic or Full-Text Data Base Services	96
6.2:	Manufacturers of Automated Circulation Systems and Number of Installations in Operation, 1981	102
6.3:	Leading Electronic Security System Marketers and Number of Installations in Operation, 1978	105
7.1:	Audiovisual Materials Sales by Product Format, 1975-1979	112
7.2	Leading Micropublishers in the Market	120
8.1:	Estimates of Public Library Spending, 1977-78 to 1983-84	128
8.2:	Estimates of Academic Library Spending, 1977-78 to 1983-84	129
8.3:	Estimates of School Library Spending, 1977-78 to 1983-84	130
8.4:	Estimates of Special Library Spending, 1978-84	131
8.5:	Estimates of Total Library Market, 1980 and 1984	132

1
Introduction

For most people, the library is a place where one can go to check out or read a book, to seek out a periodical or a microform document, obtain reference help in person or over the telephone, or even attend a community event. For a few, the library is becoming a place where one can go for professional assistance in accessing information via a hook-up to online data bases. On the horizon is the possibility of tapping into the library catalog and other community data bases from the patron's home via a personal computer. But this capability is presently available only to a handful of library users residing in prosperous high technology areas, such as the Pikes Peak Region of Colorado Springs, CO.

The economic pressures on libraries the past few years have been severe. These institutions have been caught between the rising tide of inflation and flat or declining funding support. Particularly in older urban areas, the library may have become a place of declining accessibility as hours are shortened and branches are closed. Even the prosperous Sun Belt area of California has not been immune, experiencing library closings in the wake of Proposition 13. And everywhere libraries have been fighting against rising personnel and materials costs in a variety of ways. More use has been made of nonprofessionals, volunteers and shared staff, positions have been consolidated and vacancies left unfilled. Libraries have also economized through increased sharing of resources, both materials and technological systems.

The word "library" represents a universe of more than 100,000 institutions spread throughout the United States—not to mention many thousands of libraries in other countries. For companies which sell to this market, U.S. libraries constituted a market of $1.6 billion in materials alone in 1980, out of $5.7 billion spent on all items. (See Tables 1.1, 1.2 and 1.3.)

The library market is a basic underpinning of the book and periodical publishing industries in the U.S. The more specialized the book or periodical, the more important is the library market. Thus, many scientific and technical book publishers may derive 50% or more of their sales

THE SHRINKING LIBRARY DOLLAR

from libraries, while certain publishers of scholarly journals may find that more than 80% of their subscribers are libraries.

Beyond the more commonly perceived books, periodicals and microforms, libraries represent a substantial market for audiovisual materials and equipment, for furniture and supplies, and, perhaps most exciting, for technological systems, particularly computer-based systems.

The largest category of libraries are those in elementary and high schools. Although 68% of the number of libraries are in schools, they are mostly small operations and together account for only 22% of total library spending. As shown in Table 1.1, academic libraries in colleges and universities, on the other hand, while only 3.1% of all libraries, spend almost 24% of the total budgets of all libraries.

Table 1.1: Libraries and Library Budgets in the United States, 1980

	Number	% of Total	Total Budget (millions)	% of Total
Academic	3,200	3.1%	$1,400	24.6%
Public	14,983	14.4	1,600	28.0
Special	15,000	14.4	1,300	22.8
School	70,854	68.1	1,400	24.6
Total	104,037	100.0	5,700	100.0

Source: Knowledge Industry Publications estimates, based on data from U.S. National Center for Education Statistics, Bureau of the Census, Department of Labor, Association of Research Libraries.

The estimated $1.6 billion to $2.0 billion that libraries spent on materials and equipment in 1980 is broken down in Table 1.2.

A word of caution is in order about the figures in Tables 1.1 and 1.2 as well as some of those in the rest of this report. Figures compiled by the federal government on public and academic library budgets take a considerable amount of time to be published after they are gathered and are therefore not current. No known statistics are available for special library budgets; these have been estimated on the basis of estimates of the number of special librarians (Chapter 2, Table 2.1).

While the Book Industry Study Group has done an admirable job of estimating materials acquisitions by libraries and its figures are cited throughout this report, readers should be aware that these are only estimates. Chapter 8 presents some alternative forecasts based on different assumptions about the percentage of budgets expended on materials; some of these different figures are also displayed in Table 1.2. Finally, there are no known figures on library expenditures for systems and services; these have been estimated on the basis of first-hand research and conversations with industry suppliers.

Table 1.2: Library Budgets and Estimated Acquisitions of Publications, Systems and Supplies, 1980

	Publications	Systems, All Libraries (millions)	Other,[1] All Libraries	All Materials, Systems, etc.
Academic				
Low	$ 403			
High	490			
Public				
Low	252			
High	266	not separately itemized by type of library		
Special				
Low	481			
High	501			
School				
Low	254			
High	371			
Grand Total				
Low	$1,390	$135	$50	$1,575
High	1,628	135	50	1,813

[1]Includes furniture, supplies, audiovisual equipment.
Source: Knowledge Industry Publications, based on Book Industry Study Group estimates.

CURRENT ECONOMIC TRENDS IN LIBRARIES

Chapter 2 deals in detail with the current economic situation and trends in libraries. During the 1950s and 1960s, growth in library budgets was steady and in some cases buoyant. A principal reason was growth in higher education, which meant the opening of many new colleges and the erection of new academic libraries. Expansion in elementary and secondary schools also created many new school libraries. A variety of new federal programs provided funds for academic, school and public libraries.

In the 1970s, school enrollments began dropping and higher education enrollments grew at a much slower rate. In addition, federal funds for education and library programs levelled off, failing to keep pace with in-

THE SHRINKING LIBRARY DOLLAR

flation. Some programs were actually reduced in absolute dollars. State and local budgets, the main funding source for public libraries, have also been tight, as taxpayer resistance to higher taxes forced cuts in public services, including libraries, in major cities around the U.S. As the 1980s began and Ronald Reagan was elected U.S. President, these trends were accelerating.

THE STUDY AT HAND

Libraries, as already mentioned, acquire much more than books. The bulk of this book is devoted to analyzing on a market-by-market basis what libraries buy, how they buy it and what the prospects are for growth in different components of the library market. In essence, while Tables 1.1, 1.2 and 1.3 provide the broad outline of the library market in 1980, the balance of the study fills in the details on the components of the library market as they exist now and as they will be in 1984.

The first objective of the study was to provide a comprehensive overview of libraries in the United States. Since there are a number of different kinds of libraries, specific sections are devoted to each type. In developing this material, a variety of sources were utilized for statistics, including government agencies. Discussions of certain types of libraries, i.e., academic and public, are most extensive because of the greater attention paid these institutions in the literature.

A second objective was to provide an analysis of the major components of the market: books, periodicals, audiovisual (nonprint) materials, supplies and the newest area, technological computer-based systems.

Table 1.3: Book Industry Study Group Estimates of Materials Acquisitions by All Libraries, 1980

Materials	1980 Acquisitions (millions)
Books	$ 926.7
Periodicals	436.6
Audiovisual	117.0
Microforms	50.5
Binding	55.1
	$1,585.9

Source: *Book Industry Trends*, 1980, Book Industry Study Group, Research Report No. 10, 1980.

Introduction

For purposes of clarity, the library market for books was split into two sections: general books and professional and reference books. The inherent differences in these types of books and the different ways in which they are marketed demand this separation.

A full chapter is devoted to the library market for periodicals for two reasons: first, periodicals represent a significant market and, second, library acquisitions of periodicals have affected purchase of other materials, particularly books.

A lengthy chapter has been devoted to an analysis of technological systems currently in use by libraries and being marketed by computer hardware and systems firms, both for profit and not-for-profit. Among those areas covered are cataloging and processing, online bibliographic services, automated circulation systems and book theft and security systems. This chapter also touches upon manual alternatives to computer-based systems.

While audiovisual materials, microforms and bindings represent considerably smaller percentages of library acquisitions than books and periodicals, a chapter has been devoted to them as well, concentrating on developments in their use and acquisition. Included in this chapter is a discussion of audiovisual equipment and library furniture and supplies sales.

The overall objective of this report, however, is to help libraries make informed decisions to meet the challenges ahead. By understanding the issues, trends and economic pressures affecting libraries and their most important suppliers, the publishers, libraries will be better equipped to deal with the choices that must be made—choices that may involve deployment of staff, sharing of systems or purchase of materials. There is evidence in this report, for example, that libraries, which earlier were cutting back on books in order to maintain even more costly collections of serials, are reversing that trend and increasing purchases of books. Perhaps this reversal is an informed reaction on the part of libraries to the earlier documentation of their spending patterns.

MAJOR CHALLENGES FOR LIBRARIES AND PUBLISHERS

Libraries at the beginning of the 1980s stand at the crossroad of change. Technology exists to automate and render more efficient many library services. However, these advances come at a time when library budgets are constricted, particularly in public and school institutions. Many libraries are barely able to keep up with inflation, much less explore the applications of technology for their specific needs. The advent of personal computers and various types of electronic home information services is also stirring fears that libraries may be bypassed completely, further eroding their funding support.

Several outside factors over which libraries have little or no control, and which serve to make budget problems even more severe, were injected into the library climate in the last few years.

The first came in the form of the new copyright law, which became effective January 1, 1978. In particular, Sections 107 (fair use) and 108 (limitations on exclusive rights: reproduction by libraries and archives) were of particular concern to libraries. As libraries have experienced a decline in real purchasing power of the library dollar, they have expanded their use of photocopying to provide necessary materials for patrons and (libraries said) to maintain free service.

Publishers have issued "reasonable guidelines" on photocopying, asking librarians who do copying in excess of these guidelines to pay fees to the newly established Copyright Clearance Center. National library associations like the American Library Association and Association of Research Libraries have rejected the publishers' guidelines and issued their own, which are far more lenient regarding payment of fees.

Another outside factor which has affected the library market over the past few years was the so-called taxpayer revolt, most prominently represented by the passage of Proposition 13 in California on June 6, 1978 and Proposition 2½ in Massachusets in November 1980. Many service cutbacks resulted from passage of Proposition 13, including reduction of acquisition budgets, staff positions and hours of service at libraries. The fate of public library services in an economic climate conditioned by taxpayer revolt is a major problem for this huge market.

The landslide election of Ronald Reagan as U.S. President in November 1980 on a platform promising budget cuts and tax reductions further intensified the economic plight of libraries, particularly in urban areas. A belt-tightening mentality and a thrust for cheaper government seemed pervasive.

LIMITATIONS OF THE STUDY

The first limitation was the fact that most of the large volume of published federal statistical information on libraries dates back to 1974 (academic libraries are an exception). Updates of the government studies to 1978 were in progress when this report was being prepared. Some assistance came from the National Center for Education Statistics of the U.S. Department of Education which kindly made available a portion of its unpublished statistical material.

Introduction

The dollar unit sales data and channels of distribution information gathered and now published annually by the Association of American Publishers and the Book Industry Study Group have been invaluable in the estimation of sales by library segment as well as by materials category. Nevertheless, as discussed earlier, these figures are only estimates.

This report has made the best use of existing data to describe and analyze the essential elements of the library market for publications and systems. It also draws on original data collected by Knowledge Industry Publications,Inc., especially regarding individual firms and technological developments. An impressive and long list of companies sell to the library market, as evidenced by the close to 800 exhibitors at the 1981 American Library Association annual meeting in San Francisco. As a result, efforts were made to profile firms involved in different segments of the library market. Thus, companies profiled include both large (Harcourt Brace Jovanovich) and small (Plenum Publishing) publishers, library wholesalers (Baker & Taylor and Blackwell North America, among others), companies which offer online bibliographic services (System Development Corp. and Lockheed), a giant library network (OCLC), a library subscription service (Moore-Cottrell) and a purveyor of automated circulation systems (CL Systems). Although many other companies are mentioned in the body of the report, profiles were confined to firms, important either by their size, their market share, contribution or their ability to serve as an illustration of other firms in their segment of the market.

Prospects for companies selling to the library market vary according to the company's market position and the area of library need which it serves. In general, publishers of professional and reference books will fare better in the 1980s than, for example, companies which sell audiovisual materials. General book publishers should find brighter growth prospects in the consumer market than in the library market. Library technology, still in its infancy, is expected to make substantial sales gains, but it should be noted that most systems companies start with a small sales base and are prone to technical problems which do not affect books and periodicals.

The library market is thus large but not monolithic. Its vitality is crucial for many of its suppliers, such as publishers of scholarly journals and specialist wholesalers.

Prospects for libraries and librarians in a world where their very roles may be evolving represent a challenge. Librarians are responding by reaching out for further training and library associations are stepping up their offerings of continuing education in response. As computerized systems become more widespread, the future may see fewer professional librarians in the library and more information specialists integrated into the total information environment.

In the shorter term, libraries are responding by beefing up their community information and referral role. Libraries and library directors are also paying increased attention to public relations and marketing in order to maintain or increase community support of all kinds.

2
Overview of Libraries in the U.S.

This chapter presents an overview of libraries in the United States, analyzing acquisitions, collections, expenditures, staffing and other matters by type of library: public, academic, school, special and federal. It also discusses gaps in library collections and expenditures as well as funding for libraries, a crucial problem given the reduced priorities government has given libraries in the latter half of the 1970s and early 1980s.

NUMBER OF LIBRARIES IN THE UNITED STATES

There are approximately 104,000 libraries in the United States, ranging in size from the Library of Congress to small public libraries with annual budgets of under $2000 and book funds of less than $500 annually.

Traditionally, libraries have been grouped into four categories for compiling and analyzing statistics. These are public libraries, academic libraries, school libraries and special libraries. To these categories should be added federal, or government libraries, a smaller category and one for which substantially less statistical information exists.

Public libraries are institutions supported by taxpayer funds. They have a history of almost two centuries of free service in the United States. (The 175th anniversary of the nation's first free public library was marked in 1978.) Public libraries are about 75% supported by local funds, with the balance coming from the federal government and state government, and gifts and donations. Originally repositories of books, public libraries have taken on additional functions, becoming at the same time centers for information on government programs, community service, job opportunities, education, literacy training and other tasks required by society.

Academic libraries are institutions associated with facilities for higher education, including colleges and universities, junior colleges and various advanced learning schools. They are subsidized by the institutions which they serve.

School libraries, often referred to as school library media centers, are institutions connected with elementary and high schools. As such, they are supported by taxpayer funds, or those which are earmarked for schools. The majority of public schools in the United States contain libraries.

Special libraries are institutions which serve specific professional, scientific and technical interests. They can be associated with businesses, e.g. corporate libraries such as the Chemical Bank Research Library; with schools of library science, e.g. the Columbia University School of Library Service; with specific schools or institutions of higher education, e.g. the Purdue University Mathematical Sciences Library; with societies, e.g. the Engineering Societies Library; or museums, e.g. the Metropolitan Museum of Art Library.

Knowledge Industry Publications has estimated the total universe of libraries in the United States at 104,000. The figure for school libraries comes from *Statistics of Public School Library Media Centers, 1978,* while the figure for public libraries is from an unpublished manuscript of *Public Libraries, 1977-1978;* it excludes bookmobiles and other outlets. Both reports were prepared by the National Center for Education Statistics. The 3200 figure for academic libraries is a composite from two sources, *The American Library Directory* and government figures.[1] The number of special libraries has been estimated from information from several sources, including Gale Research and the Special Libraries Association. Federal libraries are considered to be absorbed into the special libraries number.

How Americans Perceive Libraries

A 1978 study commissioned by the American Library Association, conducted by the Gallup Organization and sponsored by a special grant from Baker & Taylor, showed that Americans were generally pleased with their public library, although they were unclear about the source of support for that institution.

According to the survey, more than half of all Americans aged 18 and over had visited a public library in the last year, and 71% of library visitors had read a book in the last month. Still, about 20% of some 1515 respondents had no idea where library funding came from, and another 39% did not know that the principal source of library funding is local government.

Over half of the survey respondents indicated they almost always got what they wanted from the library; one out of four said they usually got what they wanted. The highest level of dissatisfaction noted was the availability of technical books.

Respondents generally used traditional library services most frequently. Seventy-five percent of those who had visited a library in the past year checked out a book, more than half used reference materials, almost half read newspapers or magazines. Among newer library services, respondents were most interested in "people to provide information on the phone," followed by "a computer which can be used to search for information on books you want." The concept of the library as an adjunct educational service also surfaced in the survey, with about 35% of respondents noting they would be "extremely" or "very" interested in getting help to improve their reading skills.

GROWTH IN NUMBER OF LIBRARIANS

Growth in number of librarians logically followed the growth in library facilities between 1960 and 1970, but slowed down thereafter. Table 2.1 shows that for all libraries, the number of librarians rose 67% between 1960 and 1970. The fastest rate of growth was among academic librarians, owing to the expansion of higher education and with it the number of academic libraries and collection size in this period. The number of special librarians increased 70%, school librarians 68% and public librarians 50%.

The U.S. Dept. of Labor (DOL) accurately predicted a slower rate of growth in the number of librarians between 1970 and 1980 (+23%); DOL statistics reveal that the 23% overall growth rate had been achieved by 1978. However these forecasts were not so accurate for the rates of growth of librarians by category, since the number of school and academic librarians grew slower than expected while public and special librarians growth rates exceeded expectations. The number of school librarians increased 19% between 1970 and 1978 vs. the predicted 24% by 1980; academic librarians only 28% vs. the 36% forecast. The number of public librarians grew by 24% instead of 13%, on the other hand, and special librarians by 29% vs. 18%.

The U.S. Dept. of Labor forecasts a slower rate of growth in numbers of librarians between 1978 and 1990 (+13%). Estimated increases among school and academic librarians will slow to 5% and 4% respectively. Public and special librarians are expected to continue to be the fastest growing categories although the rates will decrease somewhat.

TYPES OF LIBRARIES

Public Libraries

Public libraries are supported by government funds and exist to serve

THE SHRINKING LIBRARY DOLLAR

Table 2.1: Estimated Number of Librarians by Type of Library, 1960 and 1970; Projected Requirements, 1980 and 1990

Type of Library	1960	1970	% Change 1960-1970	Projected for 1980	% Change 1970-1980	1978	% Change 1970-1978	Projected for 1990	% Change 1978-1990
All libraries	69,000	115,000	+67%	141,000	+23%	142,000	+23%	160,000	+13%
School libraries	30,900	52,000	+68	64,500	+24	62,000	+19	65,000	+5
Academic libraries	10,400	19,500	+88	26,500	+36	25,000	+28	26,000	+4
Public libraries	17,700	26,500	+50	30,000	+13	33,000	+25	39,000	+18
Special libraries	10,000	17,000	+70	20,000	+18	22,000	+29	27,000	+23

Source: U.S. Dept. of Labor, Bureau of Labor Statistics, 1978.

the recreational and reading needs of the general public. They range downward in size, from huge institutions like the 8.8 million volume New York Public Library, to small libraries with budgets of $2000 per year.

There were 70,956 public library service outlets in the fall of 1978.[2] These were categorized as follows: 8456 central libraries, 6257 branch libraries, 49,343 bookmobiles and other mobile units and 6630 other outlets.

Close to 38,702 professional librarians staffed public libraries in 1978, comprising 41% of total staff. In addition, there were almost 48,208 support staff in clerical and technical activities (52%) and another 6424 operation and maintenance personnel (7%), making the total number of people involved in library staffing 93,334.

Table 2.2 shows that public libraries in the U.S. are and continue to be financed largely (75%) by local funds. Libraries serving smaller cities and towns, e.g. under 10,000 population, which formerly derived less of their total receipts from local sources, have now increased their funding from local, federal and especially state sources as gifts, donations and other sources have dwindled. Libraries serving larger populations of 500,000 or more have seen some decline in local funding which has been offset by small increases in gifts, donations and other sources as well as in federal and state funding.

In general, public libraries spend just over half their budgets on salaries and wages (54%), with supplies and materials the next largest category (15%). Here again, libraries serving the smallest populations, or under 10,000, differ from the average, allocating 44% of their expenditures to salaries and wages and proportionately more to supplies and materials (18%) and capital outlay (13%).

By far the largest portion of public library materials acquisitions is books, which, according to the Book Industry Study Group (BISG), acount for close to 80% of the total. However, the percentage of acquisition money spent on books is forecast to decrease from 80.2% in 1978 to 76.7% in 1984. Dollar expenditures are expected to increase 66.7% in that period, from $157.2 million to $262.1 million.

Public libraries' second largest materials expense is periodicals, which represent around 8.3% of total materials acquisitions in 1976 and 1978. That percentage was forecast to increase to 11.6% in 1984, according to BISG. Acquisitions of periodicals will rise a whopping 143.8% from $16.2 million in 1976 to $39.5 million in 1984, according to the forecast.

Binding represents a declining portion of public libraries' materials acquisitions, according to BISG, while the portions of audiovisuals and microforms will increase only slightly. However, the dollars required to

THE SHRINKING LIBRARY DOLLAR

Table 2.2: Percent of Funds and Expenditures from Various Sources for Public Libraries in Smallest and Largest Cities

	All Public (millions)	% of Total[1]	Under 10,000 Population (millions)	% of Total[1]	500,000+ Population (millions)	% of Total
Total library receipts	$1,563	100%	$124	100%	$485	100%
Local sources	1,171	75	91	73	326	67
State sources	104	7	10	8	47	10
Federal sources	123	8	8	6	43	9
Gifts, donations & other sources	166	11	16	13	69	14
Total library expenditures	1,468	100	114	100	443	100
All salaries & wages	787	54	50	44	252	57
Supplies & materials	214	15	21	18	60	14
Binding & rebinding	6	*	.7	*	2	*
Library equipment	20	1	3	3	5	1
Capital outlay	108	7	15	13	17	4
Operation & maintenance	159	11	13	11	54	12
All other	173	12	12	11	54	12

[1]May not add up to 100% due to rounding.
*Under 1%.
Source: Data from *Public Libraries 1977-78*, U.S. Department of Education, National Center for Education statistics (unpublished).

purchase both audiovisuals and microforms will increase substantially in the 1976 to 1984 period.

Table 2.3 summarizes estimated public library materials acquisitions for even years, 1976 to 1984.

By far the single most important segment of the public library market is the large urban and suburban library systems, or those serving populations of 500,000 and over. In fiscal 1978, for example, these libraries had total expenditures of $443.0 million, or one-third of the $1.4 billion spent by all public libraries. In addition, these libraries paid $254 million in salaries and wages, or 32% of the total $787 million paid in salaries and wages that year by public libraries.

Table 2.4 gives rank order of the 45 public libraries with 1 million or more volumes in their collections in 1978, while Table 2.5 provides data for 1977-1981 for 10 of the top-ranked libraries in terms of population served. In general, although total operating expenditures and library materials purchases both tend to show dollar increases, library materials purchases as a percentage of total expenditures are at best holding their own, and in most cases declining.

There are great variations in the resources offered by public libraries serving urban, suburban and non-metropolitan populations. According to the *National Inventory of Library Needs,* a 1975 study for the National Commission on Libraries and Information Science, urban libraries tend to be stronger than others in nonprint collections and acquisitions, and to be short of space. In addition, these libraries' print collections, aquisitions and operating expenditures are not at levels defined by NCLIS indicators as meeting indicated needs similar to public libraries as a whole. Also, according to the study, suburban libraries are strong in professional staffing and in nonprint collections and acquisitions, and "generally weak" in support staff. Non-metropolitan public libraries are described as strong in professional staffing, "relatively strong" in space, "especially weak" in support staff and in nonprint collections and "poorly supported" financially.

The *National Inventory* also points out distinct differences among public libraries by region. It categorizes libraries in the Northeast as "generally relatively strong, especially in nonprint materials, professional staff and acquisitions." In the Great Lakes-Plains region, the *National Inventory* says public libraries as a group are "outstanding" in professional staffing, "strong" in nonprint collections and acquisitions and "weakest" in support staff and operating budgets. In the Southeast, libraries are on the average "the weakest among the regions," while West and Southwest public libraries are "as a group strong in nonprint

THE SHRINKING LIBRARY DOLLAR

Table 2.3: Estimated Public Library Materials Acquisitions Even Years, 1976-1984
(in millions of dollars)

	1976	% of Total	1978	% of Total	1980	% of Total	1982	% of Total	1984	% of Total	% Change 1976-1984
Books	$157.2	80.2%	$188.0	80.2%	$196.0	77.9%	$221.7	77.6%	$262.1	76.7%	+ 66.7%
Periodicals	16.2	8.3	19.8	8.4	24.8	9.9	30.7	10.7	39.5	11.6	+143.8
Audiovisuals	14.3	7.3	17.2	7.3	20.3	8.1	21.6	7.6	27.7	8.1	+ 93.7
Microform	2.9	1.5	3.8	1.6	4.9	1.9	5.9	2.1	6.8	2.0	+134.5
Binding	5.5	2.8	5.6	2.4	5.7	2.3	5.7	2.0	5.8	1.7	+ 5.5
Total	$196.1	100%	$234.4	100%	$251.7	100%	$285.6	100%	$341.9	100%	+ 74.3%

Source: *Book Industry Trends*, 1980, Book Industry Study Group, Research Report No. 10, 1980.

collections and acquisitions, and they lead the other regions in adequacy of support staff."

The *National Inventory* concludes that "all of these conditions stem from very general underfunding of public libraries. A little more than $1 billion was spent in 1974 for public library operations," the study points out, "and another $1 billion would have been needed to support the libraries at per capita levels professionally regarded as necessary to provide adequate library service." It does not suggest where the extra $1 billion in funding could be found.

Analysis of Needs: Public Libraries

Gaps in staffing, collections and expenditures are facts of life for public libraries— as indeed for many public services.

While there was a substantial increase in professional staff at public libraries between 1962 and 1974, the *National Inventory* report said public libraries "were not generally better equipped to serve the needs, as measured by accepted professional criteria." According to the study, over half of public libraries' 1974 operating expenditures, or $588 million, went for salaries and wages for professional and support staff. To bring libraries not adequately staffed up to minimum levels would have required an additional $340 million, the study estimated.

Nor have public library collections kept up with needs. According to the *National Inventory,* 400 million volumes were held in 1974 when nearly 600 million were needed to meet indicated needs. While holdings of print materials grew 64% between 1962 and 1974, the aggregate need, based on population growth and needs per capita, increased 72%. The estimated total shortage in holdings in 1972 of about 100 million volumes increased to 230 million volumes by 1974. Table 2.6 shows changes in public libraries' collections between 1962 and 1974.

(Since there are no objective measures of desired library collections, these figures on collection gaps must be taken as just one opinion of library needs.)

Although public libraries' operating expenditures rose dramatically between 1962 and 1974, the *National Inventory* claimed that "indicated minimum levels of operating expenditures for adequate public library programs were achieved in 1974 by only 9% of libraries, serving 9% of the population." The study identifies libraries reaching or exceeding indicated minimum operating expenditures per capita for library services as those serving 10,000 to 100,000 people and those in jurisdictions receiving larger amounts of state and federal aid, including revenue sharing, for library purposes. It also projected the need for support in 1977

THE SHRINKING LIBRARY DOLLAR

Table 2.4: Rank Order of Public Libraries With 1 Million or More Volumes in their Collections: United States, 1974 & 1978

Library System	Rank Order 1974	Number of volumes (book stock and serials)
New York Public Library	1	8,761,899
Chicago Public Library	2	5,593,136
Los Angeles Public Library	3	4,336,734
Boston Public Library	4	3,692,569
Cleveland Public Library	5	3,146,982
Cinncinnati-Hamilton County Public Library	6	2,985,812
Free Library of Philadelphia	7	2,925,147
Queens Borough Public Library (NY)	8	2,901,274
Buffalo and Erie County Library System	9	2,839,402
Brooklyn Public Library	10	2,784,153
Milwaukee Public Library	11	2,344,914
Enoch Pratt Free Library (MD)	12	2,282,513
Detroit Public Library	13	2,255,266
Carnegie Library of Pittsburgh	14	2,120,310
Public Library of Washington, D.C.	15	1,951,756
Hawaii State Library	16	1,808,150
Houston Public Library	17	1,540,925
San Francisco Public Library	18	1,528,602
Seattle Public Library	19	1,508,950
Denver Public Library	20	1,488,350
Dallas Public Library	21	1,486,146
Public Library of Fort Wayne and Allen County (IN)	22	1,329,357
Minneapolis Public Library	23	1,303,200
St. Louis Public Library	24	1,294,251
Cuyahoga County (OH) Public Library	25	1,266,143
St. Louis County Library	26	1,215,126
San Diego Public Library	27	1,212,378
Dayton and Montgomery County Public Library (OH)	28	1,207,827
Baltimore County Public Library	29	1,173,836
Kansas City Public Library	30	1,165,505
Columbus Public Library	31	1,142,852
Memphis and Shelby County Library	32	1,126,342
Indianapolis-Marion County Library	33	1,125,375
Toledo-Lucas County Library	34	1,105,263
Public Library of Newark	35	1,096,139
King County Library (WA)	36	1,085,843
Library Association of Portland	37	1,057,667
Louisville Free Public Library	38	1,000,879

Overview of Libraries in the U.S.

Table 2.4 Rank Order of Public Libraries with 1 Million or More Volumes in their Collections: United States, 1974 & 1978 (cont.)

Library System	Rank Order 1978	Number of volumes (book stock and serials)
New York Public Library	1	
Chicago Public Library	2	6,214,748
Los Angeles Public Library	3	5,236,538
Boston Public Library	4	4,236,364
Cleveland Public Library	5	3,535,967
Queens Borough Public Library (NY)	6	3,506,309
Brooklyn Public Library	7	3,452,709
Cinncinnati-Hamilton County Public Library	8	3,318,683
Free Library of Philadelphia	9	3,040,254
Buffalo and Erie County Library System	10	3,010,577
Providence (RI)	11	2,861,937
Detroit Public Library	12	2,405,694
Enoch Pratt Free Library (MD)	13	2,375,721
Milwaukee Public Library	14	2,353,672
Carnegie Library of Pittsburgh	15	2,039,904
Houston Public Library	16	1,974,451
Public Library of Washington, D.C.	17	1,930,341
Hawaii State Library	18	1,844,423
Dallas Public Library	19	1,816,019
Cuyahoga County (OH) Public Library	20	1,804,431
Denver Public Library	21	1,709,563
San Francisco Public Library	22	1,642,683
Public Library of Fort Wayne and Allen County (IN)	23	1,512,285
Seattle Public Library	24	1,493,712
Minneapolis Public Library	25	1,454,462
Miami—Dade	26	1,426,519
St. Louis County Library	27	1,419,587
Public Library of Newark	28	1,385,496
St. Louis Public Library	29	1,364,175
Memphis and Shelby County Library	30	1,358,026
Montgomery County (MD)	31	1,313,061
Dayton and Montgomery County Public Library (OH)	32	1,302,269
Indianapolis-Marion County Library	33	1,285,152
Toledo-Lucas County Library	34	1,255,038
Baltimore County Public Library	35	1,220,679
Library Association of Portland	36	1,191,870
Kansas City Public Library	37	1,186,484
Fairfax County (VA)	38	1,180,190
Prince George (MD)	39	1,169,173
Columbus Public Library	40	1,164,423
King County Library (WA)	41	1,127,393
Phoenix Public Library	42	1,088,095
Mid-Continent (MO)	43	1,077,405
Atlanta Public Library	44	1,033,507
Orange County (CA)	45	1,029,148

Source: Unpublished manuscript of *Public Libraries 1977-78*, U.S. Department of Education, National Center for Education Statistics.

THE SHRINKING LIBRARY DOLLAR

Table 2.5: Expenditures of 10 Large Public Libraries, 1977-1981

Library	Population (millions)				Total Expenditures (millions)				
	77	78	79	80	81	77	78	79	80	81
Chicago	3.4	3.4	3.4	3.4	NA	$22.2	$26.1	$25.1	$28.6	$31.7
New York	3.3	3.3	3.3	3.3	NA	23.1	27.5	29.8	30.2	33.0
Los Angeles	2.8	2.8	2.9	3.0	3.0	16.7	16.5	18.2	20.8	23.9
Brooklyn	2.3	2.3	2.2	2.2	2.2	14.1	16.7	17.0	16.0	18.0
Queens Borough	2.0	2.0	2.0	2.0	NA	18.6	19.1	20.5	20.4	22.0
Free Library of Philadelphia	2.0	2.0	2.0	2.0	2.0	17.3	20.5	19.4	21.4	21.1
Detroit	1.5	1.5	1.5	1.5	NA	11.0	12.4	13.8	14.1	14.8
Buffalo/Erie	1.1	1.1	1.1	1.1	NA	7.1	9.7	10.0	10.5	10.8
Miami/Dade	1.1	1.1	1.3	1.3	1.3	9.0	8.5	10.6	12.5	14.3
Milwaukee	.9	.9	.9	1.0	1.0	5.8	8.4[1]	8.5	9.1	9.9

Overview of Libraries in the U.S.

Table 2.5: Expenditures of 10 Large Public Libraries, 1977-1981 (cont.)

Library	Library Material Expenditures (millions)						% of Library Materials to Total Expenditures				
	77	78	79	80	81		77	78	79	80	81
Chicago	$2.5	$3.2	$2.6	$4.6	$4.7		11.3%	12.3%	10.4%	16.1%	14.8%
New York	3.1	3.7	3.7	3.5	3.7		13.6	13.6	12.5	11.6	11.2
Los Angeles	2.7	2.8	3.0	3.4	4.0		16.2	17.0	16.5	16.3	16.7
Brooklyn	2.3	2.1	2.3	2.5	2.3		16.3	12.6	13.5	15.6	12.8
Queens Borough	2.1	2.3	2.9	2.8	2.9		11.3	12.0	14.1	13.7	13.2
Free Library of Philadelphia	1.8	2.1	1.8	2.0	1.5		10.4	10.2	9.9	9.4	7.3
Detroit	.7	1.1	1.2	1.0	.8		6.0	9.0	9.0	7.0	5.0
Buffalo/Erie	.9	1.1	1.1	1.1	1.2		12.7	11.3	11.0	10.5	11.1
Miami/Dade	2.3	1.7	1.7	2.1	2.4		25.1	20.0	16.0	16.8	16.8
Milwaukee	.8	.8	.9	.9	1.0		13.8	9.5	10.6	9.9	10.1

[1] First year fringe benefits included.
NA: Not available.
Source: Knowledge Industry Publications, Inc.

THE SHRINKING LIBRARY DOLLAR

and thereafter as well over the $2 billion indicated for 1974, based on population increase, service extensions to populations not served in 1974, per-patron usage increases, higher costs of books and films and salary scale adjustments.

Table 2.7 gives public libraries' operating expenditures in 1962 and 1974. The trend since 1962 does show that these libraries are gaining in the percentage of minimum needs that is available—from 42% in 1962 to 49% in 1974.

Even though public library expenditures continue to climb steadily, increasing almost 5.3% in 1979 according to one source[3], materials expenditures accounted for only 16% of this total compared to 68% for salaries. In addition, as illustrated in Table 2.5, large public libraries are often spending a declining percentage of total expenditures on materials. This is a significant finding, since the 10 libraries tracked in Table 2.5 spent a total of $19.2 million in 1977, $20.9 million in 1978, $21.2 million in 1979, $23.9 million in 1980 and $24.5 million in 1981, representing 8.9% of estimated public library material acquisitions in 1976, 8.9% in 1977, 8.9% in 1978, 8.8% in 1979, 9.5% in 1980 and 9.0% in 1981.

Academic Libraries

Academic libraries include those at colleges and universities, junior colleges and law, medical and religious schools. There are roughly 3000

Table 2.6: Public Library Collections, 1962 and 1974

	1962	1974	% Change
Number of libraries	6565	8307	26.5%
Book collections (in millions of volumes)	NA	387.6	—
Total print materials held (millions of volumes equivalent)	241.4	397.0	64.5
Indicated minimum print volumes needed (in millions)	343.4	591.4	72.2
Shortage in print materials (in millions)	102.0	229.6	125.1
Audiovisual materials held (thousands)	NA	8309	NA
All other materials held (thousands)	NA	37,268	NA
Nonprint materials held (thousands)	NA	45,577	NA
Indicated minimum nonprint materials needed (thousands)	NA	19,110	NA
Shortage in nonprint materials (thousands)	NA	10,718	NA

NA: Not available.
Source: *National Inventory of Library Needs, 1975.*

Overview of Libraries in the U.S.

Table 2.7: Public Library Operating Expenditures, 1962 and 1974

	1962	1974	% Change
Operating expenditures (millions)	$317	$1,018	221.0%
Population served (millions)	155.7	198.6	27.6
Minimum operating expenditures needed (millions)	756	1,977	162.0
Shortage (millions)[1]	439	1,004	129.0
Percentage of minimum expenditures available	41.9	49.2	17.4
Operating expenditures per capita (average)	2.04	5.13	151.0
Percentage of population served by libraries not meeting expected per capita operating expenditures	NA	91	NA
Operating expenditures in 1965 dollars (millions of dollars)	798	1,544	93.0
Operating expenditures per capita in 1965 dollars	2.15	7.78	262.0

[1]Since many jurisdictions support libraries to provide services above the minimum levels, the sum of the shortages in other libraries is greater than the difference between aggregate minimum operating expenditures needed and the total actual operating expenditures.
NA: Not available.
Source: *National Inventory of Library Needs, 1975.*

college, university and junior college libraries in the U.S. Adding law, medical and religious libraries which are part of university systems brings the total to well over 3200.[4]

These institutions can range from small, junior college libraries with collections of just a few thousand books to giants such as Harvard University's 9.4 million volume library. Table 2.8 gives selected statistics on the collections, staff and operating expenditures of the 10 largest academic libraries in 1976 and 1977.

Table 2.8 ranks libraries by number of volumes. Interestingly, if the ranking were done on the basis of expenditures for books and other library materials, positions would shift dramatically. Rank in spending for 1976-1977 would find the Universtiy of Texas (Austin) first, ahead of Harvard, the library with the largest number of volumes. It would move Stanford, ranked seventh in number of volumes, to third place ahead of Yale, ranked second by volumes. Table 2.9 gives rank by material expenditures.

Again, the University of Texas (Austin) spent proportionately more of its total operating budget on materials than any other library, with $3.8

THE SHRINKING LIBRARY DOLLAR

Table 2.8: Selected Statistics on Collections, Staff and Operating Expenditures of the 10 Largest Academic Libraries, 1976-77

Institution or Branch	Number of Volumes	Total	Salaries, Wages, Fringe Benefits	Books and Other Library Materials	Binding and Rebinding	All Other Operating Expenditures
Harvard University	9,547,576	$14,362,801	$9,101,183	$3,262,000	$436,701	$1,562,917
Yale University	6,884,604	11,225,498	7,177,888	2,434,317	226,631	1,386,662
University of Illinois (Urbana)	5,494,786	7,353,119	4,551,833	2,210,425	160,264	430,597
University of Michigan (Ann Arbor)	4,917,381	9,336,782	6,176,489	2,341,978	207,954	610,361
University of California (Berkeley)	4,917,330	11,779,605	8,590,185	2,255,075	278,315	656,030
Columbia University (main division)	4,716,162	8,247,083	6,454,647	1,640,032	152,404	0
Stanford University	4,170,325	11,178,908	6,401,918	2,882,493	270,318	1,624,179
University of California (Los Angeles)	3,908,053	11,746,071	8,087,531	2,022,313	417,977	1,218,250
University of Chicago	3,886,130	6,155,418	3,187,603	1,394,989	169,036	1,403,790
University of Texas (Austin)	3,713,821	9,319,210	4,990,945	3,794,931	106,092	427,242

Source: U.S. Dept. of Education, National Center for Education Statistics, *Library Statistics of Colleges and Universities, 1977 Institutional Data.*

Table 2.9: Leading Academic Libraries Ranked by Expenditures for Materials, 1976-77

Institution or Branch	Books and Other Library Materials Expenditures	Materials Expenditures as % of Total
University of Texas (Austin)	$3,794,931	40.7%
Harvard University	3,262,000	22.7
Stanford University	2,882,493	25.8
Yale University	2,434,317	21.7
University of Michigan (Ann Arbor)	2,341,978	25.1
University of California (Berkeley)	2,255,075	19.1
University of Illinois (Urbana)	2,210,425	30.1
University of California (Los Angeles)	2,022,313	17.2
Columbia University (main division)	1,640,032	19.9
University of Chicago	1,394,989	22.7

Source: U.S. Dept. of Education, National Center for Education Statistics, *Library Statistics of College and Universities, 1977 Institutional Data.*

million of $9.2 million, or 40.7%, going for materials. Harvard's percentage of material expenditures to total expenditures was more typical, 22.7%.

Academic libraries also vary widely in terms of function served, which ranges from providing material that is related to specific college courses to supplying material for in-depth research in many academic fields at large universities. At many of these large universities, undergraduate libraries have been separated from the large research collections to make it easier for students to use the libraries for their studies.

Table 2.10, which provides a detailed breakdown of academic library statistics in the 1970s, shows that these institutions grew rapidly in that decade, along with enrollments. The number of academic libraries rose 20.6% from 2535 in 1970-1971 to 3058 in 1976-1977.

Collections also grew substantially, with number of volumes up 29.6% from 371 million to 481 million. The number of periodicals increased from 3.7 million to 4.7 million, up 27.0%, and total library staff proliferated, rising from 48,953 in 1970-1971 to 57,087 in 1976-1977, a 16.6% increase.

THE SHRINKING LIBRARY DOLLAR

Library operating expenditures, excluding capital outlays, also experienced rapid growth in the 1970s, going from a total of $737.5 million in 1970-1971 to $1.3 billion in 1976-1977, a 70.8% increase. Despite the large percentage increase in expenditures, however, library operating expenditures as a percentage of total institutional expenditures for education and general purposes remained flat at 3.2%.

A number of factors fueled the growth of academic libraries in the 1970s. One was the dramatic rise in number of college students in this decade, from 8.6 million in 1970 to 11.6 million in fall 1978. Second, federal programs, especially in the 1960s, helped spur library materials purchases. These programs, including the Higher Education Act of 1965, encouraged libraries to buy a variety of new types of materials and services, including cassettes, films, microforms, etc.

Two important trends should be noted about academic libraries in the 1970s. First, despite increases in expenditures for materials and personnel, rising costs continue to erode the capabilities of academic libraries to build collections and provide services. Table 2.11 shows that while total operating expenditures in one group of libraries rose 172% between 1973-1974 and 1979-1980, the number of volumes in these libraries grew just 59% in this period and the number of total staff was up only 40%. Salaries and wages, on the other hand, increased 156%.

Second, the expected shift of dollars from book to periodical purchases has not occurred. According to Book Industry Group figures, periodicals took an estimated 32.9% of the acquisitions budget in 1980, down from 34.0% in 1976. The books' share rose from 52.1% to 55.1% in that period. The books' share will rise further to 59.4% in 1984, while that of periodicals will decrease to 30.0%.

Statistics gathered by the Association of Research Libraries (ARL) over the period from 1973-1974 to 1979-1980 (Table 2.11) also refute the conventional wisdom that periodicals eat up ever increasing portions of library budgets. ARL figures show that the percentage of total library expenditures spent on current periodicals rose only from 10.0% to 11.4% from 1976-1977 to 1979-1980. The percentage of total expenditures spent on library materials, which includes books and serials, remained almost constant at about 23.0%. ARL figures also reveal that academic library growth has slowed. While volumes increased 42% from 1973-1974 to 1976-1977, the period from 1976-1977 to 1979-1980 showed only a 12% increase. Total microform units and current serials exhibited strong growth over the entire seven year period. Professional staff, up sharply in the early 1970s, actually decreased in the latter part of the decade, while expenditures for salaries rose 156%.

Overview of Libraries in the U.S.

Total academic library materials acquisitions are projected to rise about 76% in dollars between 1976 and 1984. Books will represent the fastest growing segment of the market, according to projections made by the Book Industry Study Group, rising 100%. Periodicals will increase 54%. Audiovisual material acquisitions will drop, and microforms and bindings will both increase, with microforms posting a 62.9% increase. Despite the positive outlook for dollar sales, book units will rise only 19.2% and periodical units will decrease 30.0% in this eight-year period. Table 2.12 illustrates trends in dollar sales.

Analysis of Needs: Academic Libraries

The *National Inventory of Library Needs—1975* reported that academic libraries' operating expenditures increased 403% between 1963 and 1975. As shown in Table 2.13 expenditures far outstripped the growth in numbers of libraries and students. The study said 77% of academic libraries were not meeting "indicated expenditures."

School Libraries

A 1978 survey by the National Center for Education Statistics (NCES) put the number of public school library/media centers at 70,854, down from 74,625 in 1974. Of the 1978 total, 74% were elementary and combined school libraries while the balance were in secondary schools.

Together these libraries served 40.6 million pupils, 8% less than in 1974, and had total operating expenditures of almost $1.4 billion, or $34.12 per pupil in public school enrollment. Table 2.14 breaks down these expenses, by purpose and by level of school.

Full time equivalent (FTE) staff in schools in 1978 totaled 84,414, including 52,256 in elementary and combined facilities and the balance, or 32,158 in secondary libraries. This figure compares with a total of 101,465 reported in 1974. Certified staff comprise 95% of the FTE staff in 1978 or 80,193 vs. 62% in 1974 or 62,908. Full time equivalent staff was down 16.8% 1974-1978.

School library/media centers housed more than 520 million volumes in their print collections in 1974, including books, bound periodicals and microforms. In addition, their collections included some 97 million titles, and 68 million audiovisual materials. School library/media centers spent $191 million for print acquisitions and $87 million for nonprint acquisitions in 1974. Table 2.15 shows that school libraries acquired 39.9 million books and bound periodicals in 1974 as well as 194,000 microform titles. The books acquired amounted to 7.6% of total

THE SHRINKING LIBRARY DOLLAR

Table 2.10: General Statistics of College and University Libraries, and Outlying Areas, 1970-71, 1975-76 and 1976-77

	1970-71	1972-73	1974-75	1975-76	1976-77	% Change 1970-71–1975-76	% Change 1970-71–1976-77	% Change 1972-73–1976-77
Number of libraries	2,535	2,908	2,972	2,984	3,058	+17.7 %	+20.6%	+5.2%
Number of students enrolled, total (thousands)	8,649	9,298	10,322	11,291	11,600	+30.5	+34.1	+24.8
Collections (thousands of units)								
Number of volumes at end of year	371,389	406,790	447,059	467,934	481,442	+26.0	+29.6	+18.4
Number of volumes added during year	26,374	25,095	23,242	22,943	23,367	−13.0	−15.2	−10.9
Number of periodical titles at end of year	3,677	3,806	4,434	4,616	4,670	+25.5	+27.0	+22.7
Library staff in terms of full-time equivalents								
Total staff in regular positions	48,953	53,876	56,836	56,827	57,087	+16.1	+16.6	+6.0
Professional library staff	21,886	23,067	23,530	23,089	23,308	+5.5	+6.5	+1.0
Nonprofessional library staff	27,068	30,809	33,306	33,738	33,779	+24.6	+24.8	+9.6
Hours of student and other assistance (thousands)	37,385	33,599	34,687	36,720	39,950	−1.8	+6.9	+18.9

Overview of Libraries in the U.S.

Library operating expenditures (excluding capital outlay) in thousands of dollars								
Operating expenditures, total	$737,533	$866,838	$1,091,784	$1,180,128	$1,259,637	+60.0	+70.8	+45.3
Salaries	361,295	443,296	592,568	649,374	698,090	+79.7	+93.2	+57.5
Hourly wages	56,052	53,250	61,474	66,175	68,683	+18.1	+22.5	+29.0
Binding and rebinding	19,781	20,813	22,206	22,375	22,521	+13.1	+13.9	+8.2
Books and other library materials	247,668	282,195	327,904	357,544	373,699	+44.4	+50.9	+32.4
Other library operating expenditures	52,737	67,284	87,632	84,660	96,643	+60.5	+83.3	+43.6
Operating expenditures in percents, total	100%	100%	100%	100%	100%			
Salaries	49	51	54	55	55			
Hourly wages	7	6	6	6	5			
Binding and rebinding	3	2	2	2	2			
Books and other library materials	34	33	30	30	30			
Other library operating expenditures	7	8	8	7	8			

Source: U.S. Dept. of Health, Education and Welfare, National Center for Education Statistics, *Library Statistics of Colleges and Universities*, various reports.

THE SHRINKING LIBRARY DOLLAR

Table 2.11: Academic Library Statistics, 1973-1974, 1976-1977 and 1979-1980

	1973-74[1]	% of Total	1976-77[2]	% of Total	% Change 1973-74—1976-77	1979-80[3]	% of Total	% Change 1976-1977—1979-1980	% Change 1973-1976—1979-1980
Collections (millions)									
Volumes in library	167.7		238.5		+42%	266.2		+12%	+59%
Volumes added (gross)	7.5		9.0		+20	8.5		−6	+13
Volumes added (net)	6.6		7.9		+20	7.6		−4	+15
Total microform units	61.5		106.6		+73	146.7		+38	+139
Current serials	2.1		2.7		+29	4.9		+81	+133
Expenditures (millions)									
Library materials	$ 94.5	29.7%	$145.4	23.2%	+54	200.4	23.1%	+38	+12
Current periodicals	NA	—	62.7	10.0	—	98.9	11.4	+57	—
Binding	9.0	2.8	12.5	2.0	+39	15.1	1.7	+21	+68
Total materials & binding	103.5	32.5	157.9	25.2	+53	215.4	24.8	+36	+108
Total salaries & wages	189.1	59.4	378.9	60.5%	+100	485.0	55.9	+28	+156
Other operating expenditures	25.9	8.1	88.9	14.2	+243	167.3	19.3	+88	+546
Total library operating expenditures	318.5		625.8		+96	867.6		+39	+172
Personnel									
Professional	6.7		11.6		+73	10.9		−6	+63
Nonprofessional	13.3		17.5		+32	19.8		+13	+49
Student	5.0		5.8		+16	6.3		+9	+26
Total	25.0		35.0		+40	37.0		+6	+48

[1] Based on 82 members.
[2] Based on 105 members.
[3] Based on 111 members.
Source: *Academic Library Statistics*, 1973-1974, 1976-1977 and 1979-1980 editions.

Overview of Libraries in the U.S.

Table 2.12: Estimated Academic Library Materials Expenditures, Even Years, 1976-1984

	1976	% of Total	1978	% of Total	1980 (millions)	% of Total	1982	% of Total	1984	% of Total	% Change 1976-1984
Books	$201.2	52.1%	$234.1	53.8%	$269.6	55.1%	$341.1	57.7%	$404.3	59.4%	+100.9%
Periodicals	131.5	34.0	145.6	33.5	161.0	32.9	182.2	30.9	203.7	30.0	+54.9
Audiovisuals	15.3	4.0	13.7	3.1	11.3	2.3	11.5	2.0	13.1	1.9	−14.4
Microforms	15.9	4.1	17.9	4.1	20.6	4.2	23.7	4.0	25.9	3.8	+62.9
Binding	22.4	5.8	23.7	5.4	27.1	5.5	30.7	5.2	33.1	4.9	+47.8
Total	$386.3	100%	$435.0	100%	$489.6	100%	$589.2	100%	$680.1	100%	+76.1%

Source: *Book Industry Trends, 1980*, Book Industry Study Group, Research Report No. 10, 1980.

Table 2.13: Operating Expenditures of Academic Libraries, 1963 and 1975

	1963	1975	% Change
Number of libraries	2075	3026	46%
Number of students served (millions)	4.3	10.2	135
Operating expenditures (millions)	$213	$1071	403

Source: *National Inventory of Library Needs, 1975*.

31

THE SHRINKING LIBRARY DOLLAR

Table 2.14: Expenditures for Public School Libraries by Purpose and Level of School, 1974 and 1978

	Elementary & Combined Schools 1974	Elementary & Combined Schools 1978	Secondary Schools 1974	Secondary Schools 1978	All Schools 1974	All Schools 1978	All Schools % Change 1974-1978
	(thousands)						
Total expenditures	$636,390	$834,744	$545,890	$550,864	$1,182,280	$1,385,608	+ 17.2%
Salaries & wages	441,660	611,247	376,660	389,303	818,320	1,000,550	+ 22.3
Books	86,860	106,199	76,100	66,274	162,960	172,473	+ 5.8
Audiovisual materials	47,870	40,409	42,570	28,012	90,440	68,421	− 24.3
Audiovisual equipment	38,440	33,132	28,010	23,502	66,450	56,634	− 14.8
Periodicals	10,560	14,054	14,310	15,958	24,870	30,012	+ 20.7
All other	11,000	29,703	8,240	27,815	19,240	57,518	+199.0

Source: *Public School Library Media Centers Survey of 1978*, U.S. Department of Education, Washington, DC, National Center for Education Statistics.

Overview of Libraries in the U.S.

Table 2.15: School Library/Media Center Collections and Acquisitions, 1974

	Elementary & Combined Schools	Secondary Schools	All Schools
Number of libraries	52,310	22,315	74,625
Number of pupils (millions)	25.3	18.6	43.9
Print materials collections			
Total volumes of books & bound periodicals (millions)	270.7	176.6	447.3
Total volumes (including microform equivalent) (millions)	313.1	208.6	521.7
Volumes of books & bound periodicals acquired in 1974 (millions)	22.9	16.9	39.9
Microform titles acquired in 1974 (thousands)	76.0	118.0	194.0
Total volumes acquired in 1974 (millions)	23.0	17.0	40.1
Audiovisual and other materials			
Total A/V titles in 1974 (millions)	43.7	24.3	68.0
Total, all other titles (millions)	17.1	11.7	28.7
Total titles (millions)	60.8	36.0	96.7
A/V titles acquired in 1974 (thousands)	4,901	2,997	7,898
All other titles acquired in 1974 (thousands)	1,793	1,556	3,349
Total titles acquired in 1974 (thousands)	6,694	4,553	11,248
Expenditures in 1974 for collection			
Books, periodicals, microforms (millions)	$98	$93	$191
Audiovisual and other materials (millions)	47	40	87

Source: *National Inventory of Library Needs, 1975.*

volumes in the collection. Additions of audiovisual materials in 1974 equaled 11.6% of total collection size.

Federal statistics on school library/media expenditures for 1978 show that the school library/media center market for books became depressed in the mid-1970s. During the four years from 1974 to 1978, total expenditures for public school libraries increased only 17%, those for books 5.8% while expenditures for audiovisual materials and equipment decreased sharply. A number of factors mitigated against acquisitions of books and audiovisual materials. These include declining enrollments, tight local school budgets, consolidation of facilities, taxpayers' resistance to education costs, lower federal funding and higher teachers' salaries.

Studies done for the Book Industry Study Group (Darien, CT), a not-for-profit industry research organization, predicted earlier that this depressed state will continue in the 1980s, as school libraries remain caught between tight acquisition dollars and higher prices of desired materials. In 1978, BISG estimated that materials acquisition expenditures by school libraries would be 14% lower in 1982 than in 1974, with audiovisual acquisitions showing the greatest decline among the three largest categories. However, the latest BISG study predicts total acquisitions to rise nearly 60% from 1976 to 1984, with expenditures on books showing a 92% increase and periodicals 62%. Audiovisual and microform materials will decline 15% and 17% respectively, according to the 1980 BISG study. That a good part of the dollar increase is due to price inflation is revealed by the unit forecast which shows periodical units actually decreasing by 5%. Book units will rise an estimated 31%, while audiovisual units will shrink 55.5%, according to BISG. Table 2.16 summarizes this information.

Special Libraries

Statistics on special libraries are as scarce as data on public, school and academic libraries are profuse. However, there are scattered statistics from various places which give some estimate of the number of special libraries.

The *1981 Directory of Special Libraries* (Gale) estimates the number of special libraries at over 15,000. In the fourth quarter of 1978, the Special Libraries Association (SLA) itself reported 11,600 members. The 1980 edition of *The Bowker Annual of Library and Book Trade Information* puts the number of special libraries much lower, at 9652.

Overview of Libraries in the U.S.

Table 2.16: Estimates of School Library Acquisitions, Even Years, 1976-1984

	1976	% of Total	1978	% of Total	1980	% of Total	1982	% of Total	1984	% of Total	% Change 1976-1984
Books	$186.9	63.6%	$226.4	68.3%	$264.1	71.2%	$302.8	73.4%	$359.2	76.1%	+92.2%
Periodicals	27.6	9.4	30.5	9.2	34.6	9.3	39.2	9.5	44.8	9.5	+62.3
Audiovisuals	78.4	26.7	73.4	22.1	71.3	19.2	69.4	16.8	67.0	14.2	−14.5
Microforms	0.6	0.2	0.6	0.2	0.6	0.2	0.5	0.1	0.5	0.1	−16.7
Binding	0.5	0.2	0.5	0.2	0.5	0.1	0.5	0.1	0.5	0.1	—
	$294.0	100%[1]	$331.4	100%[1]	$371.1	100%	$412.4	100%[1]	$472.0	100%	+60.5

[1]May not add up to 100% due to rounding.
Source: *Book Industry Trends, 1980*, Book Industry Study Group, Research Report No. 10, 1980.

Table 2.17: Estimates of Special Library Acquisitions, Even Years, 1976-1984

	1976	% of Total	1978	% of Total	1980	% of Total	1982	% of Total	1984	% of Total	% Change 1976-1984
Books	$106.8	40.5%	$154.7	41.0%	$197.3	39.4%	$252.4	41.5%	$304.1	42.8%	+184.7%
Periodicals	118.4	44.9	173.3	46.0	243.2	48.6	288.1	47.3	332.4	46.8	+180.7
Audiovisuals	10.3	3.9	12.5	3.3	14.1	2.8	15.5	2.5	16.1	2.3	+56.3
Microforms	13.3	5.0	18.1	4.8	24.4	4.9	28.2	4.6	29.7	4.2	+123.3
Bindings	14.7	5.6	17.8	4.7	21.8	4.4	24.3	4.0	27.8	3.9	+89.1
	$263.5	100%[1]	$376.4	100%[1]	$500.8	100%[1]	$608.5	100%[1]	$710.1	100%[1]	+169.5

[1]May not add up to 100% due to rounding.
Source: *Book Industry Trends, 1980*, Book Industry Study Group, Research Report No. 10, 1980.

THE SHRINKING LIBRARY DOLLAR

There is a variety of types of special libraries, including those connected with businesses, such as Hewlett Packard Co. Libraries (Palo Alto, CA) and Chemical Bank Research Library (New York, NY); those connected with medical, law and library schools, e.g. Washington & Lee Law School Library (Lexington, VA) and the Universtiy of Texas Graduate School of Library Science (Austin, TX), and those connected with historical, legislative and research institutions, e.g. the Library of Congress Prints and Photographs Division (Washington, DC).

According to SLA, many of its 11,600 members represent small facilities with only one or two full-time librarians. This means that gatherings of special librarians present significant marketing and sales opportunities for those who sell to the library market, since these staff members are much more likely to make on-the-spot purchasing decisions than, for example, the more diverse body of librarians attending the annual American Library Association convention. At the other end of the spectrum from these small libraries is an institution such as the Engineering Societies Library (ESL), a technical institution which contains 250,000 volumes, has 1800 periodical subscriptions and a $145,000 acquisition budget and acts as a subject referral library for engineering technology information. The library also receives $50,000 of free periodicals and $77,000 of free monographs for review purposes and as the supply arm of the abstracting service, Engineering Index. In its 1980 fiscal year, ESL added 7600 volumes, only 1000 more than the previous year and at double the expense, according to S.K. Cabeen, ESL library director.

Table 2.17 shows estimated special library purchases of $263.5 million in 1976, a figure which was projected to rise to $710.1 million in 1984 by the Book Industry Study Group. Periodical acquisitions will show the largest dollar gain; they will also show an increase in unit sales in that period (see also Chapter 5). Book acquisitions, while not showing such a large gain in dollars, will actually reflect a larger gain in unit purchases, according to BISG. Special libraries are also an excellent market for online computer data bases, because searches of such bases can often be paid for from a company research budget.

Federal Libraries

The number of federal libraries in 1978 was 2142, which included three national libraries (Library of Congress, National Library of Medicine, National Agricultural Library) and 2139 other federal libraries. Table 2.18, which gives a breakdown of these libraries by collection, circulation, operating expenditures, etc., shows that the operating expenditures

Overview of Libraries in the U.S.

Table 2.18: Statistics of Federal Libraries, FY 1972 and FY 1978

	FY 1972 Total	1972 National	All Other Federal	FY 1978 Total	1978 National	All Other Federal	Selected % of Change 1972-1978 Total	National	All Other Federal
Number of libraries	2,145	3	2,142	2,142	3	2,139			
Total volumes, books and periodicals in collections (millions)	59.9	18.5	41.4	67.2	26.2	41.1	+ 12.2%	+ 41.6%	
Circulation (millions)	45.0	2.4	42.6	40.8	2.3	38.5			
Total operating expenditures (millions)	$191.8	$95.6	$96.3	$516.5	$185.5	$331.1	+ 169.3%	+ 94.0%	+ 243.8%
Salaries	121.9	61.1	60.8	317.0	95.8	221.2	+ 160.0	+ 56.8	+ 263.8
Library materials	38.7	11.3	27.4	74.1	6.9	67.1	+ 91.5	− 38.9	+ 144.9
Other operating expenditures	31.2	23.2	8.1	125.5	82.7	42.7	+ 302.2	+ 256.5	+ 427.2
Total employees	11,080	4,119	6,961	20,196	5,194	15,002	+ 82.3	+ 26.1	+ 130.5
Professional employees	3,209	1,019	2,190	6,356	2,447	3,909			

Note: Not all libraries responded to detailed categories.
Source: U.S. Office of Health, Education and Welfare, National Center for Education Statistics *Survey of Federal Libraries, 1972* and U.S. Office of Education, National Center for Education Statistics Federal Library Committee. Unpublished data for FY 1978.

THE SHRINKING LIBRARY DOLLAR

of the three national libraries were about the same as those of the 2139 other federal libraries at the time of the 1972 survey, although the trio of national libraries spent substantially less on materials than the other institutions combined, $11.3 million vs. $27.4 million in that year. By 1978, operating expenditures of all other federal libraries were 78.5% higher than those of the three national libraries and expenditures for library materials $67.1 million vs. $6.9 million for the national libraries. Materials acquisitions for the national libraries actually decreased by 38.9% from 1972 to 1978.

FUNDING FOR LIBRARIES

Public and school libraries grew at a rapid clip in the 1960s and early 1970s, due in large measure to the infusion of federal funds from "Great Society" programs. Academic libraries followed the trend of the other libraries, as higher education expanded rapidly. Much of this growth slowed in the 1970s, however, as federal funding for some programs dried up and consolidation of programs diverted funds away from libraries. At the state and local levels, fiscal constraints also diverted funds away from libraries, which traditionally receive only a tiny percentage of government funds in comparison with other services such as education, health and hospitals, etc.

Although public libraries derive the bulk of their revenues from local sources, the state role in support of these institutions has expanded in the 1970s. Table 2.19 shows that the state share rose from 10.8% in 1972 to 12.9% in 1975, at the same time its share of public education funding was rising from 40.2% to 43.6%.

In general, libraries do not fare well in competition for the local tax dollar. Table 2.20 compares expenditures for selected state and local government functions between 1972-1973, 1975-1976 and 1978-1979, and illustrates that while funding for the four functions increased at about the same rate from 1972-1973 to 1975-1976, funding for libraries was only a minute portion of the total, 1.3% in both years. By 1978-1979, funding for libraries had decreased to only 1.2% of the total. Moreover, funding for hospitals showed a dramatic rate of increase over the other three functions between 1975-1976 and 1978-1979, while funding for police also increased more rapidly than for libraries and local schools.

In terms of dollars, the two largest federal programs for libraries are ESEA IV-B (Elementary and Secondary Education Act) and the Library Services and Construction Act. Title IV-B represents the consolidation created by the Education Amendments of 1974 of Title II of ESEA

Overview of Libraries in the U.S.

Table 2.19: Percentage Distribution of Expenditures for Public Libraries and Public Schools, 1972, 1974 and 1975

		Federal	State	Local
Public Libraries	1972	5.8%	10.8%	83.4%
	1974	4.3	12.4	83.3
	1975	5.0	12.9	82.1
Public Schools	1972	8.0	40.2	51.8
	1974	8.2	42.6	49.2
	1975	7.8	43.6	48.6

Source: *Improving State Aid to Public Libraries, 1977.* National Commission on Libraries and Information Science.

(guidance, counseling, testing) with Title III of the National Defense Education Act (educational equipment, minor remodeling). Title IV-B funds are now used for purposes which previously had been funded by the separate acts, i.e. acquisition of school library resources and instructional equipment, and minor remodeling of space used for such equipment and guidance, counseling and testing. A current proposal by the Reagan administration may see these funds lumped into block grants and spent however the recipient wishes.

The Library Services and Construction Act (LSCA), extended for five years in 1977, provides funds for library services under a number of titles, including Title I (library services), Title II (construction) and Title III (interlibrary cooperation). Although LSCA programs fared slightly better under the Carter administration than in the lean Nixon-Ford years, the increase has not been enough to do more than hold steady in the face of inflation. Table 2.21 summarizes federal funding for libraries for fiscal 1977, through fiscal 1981. This table also furnishes President Reagan's budget proposals for fiscal 1982 which slash or lump funding for federal library programs into a single and reduced block grant where funds may not be specified for libraries. The Reagan budget proposes zero funding for the college library program and cuts 25% from both school and public library programs.

The impact of general revenue sharing funds, which commenced following enactment of the State and Local Fiscal Assistance Act of 1972, added a new dimension to federal aid to libraries. Under this act, local governments could use their share of general revenue sharing on eight priority expenditure categories, of which libraries are one.

THE SHRINKING LIBRARY DOLLAR

Table 2.20: General State and Local Government Expenditures for Selected Areas, 1972-73, 1975-76 and 1978-79

	1972-73	1975-76	% Change 1972-73 and 1975-76 (millions)	1978-79	% Change 1975-76 and 1978-79	% Change 1972-73 and 1978-79
Local schools	$48,789	$67,674	+38.7%	$ 83,385	+23.2%	+70.9%
Hospitals	11,112	15,726	+41.5	28,218	+79.4	+153.9
Police	6,710	9,531	+42.0	12,208	+28.1	+81.9
Libraries	877	1,249	+42.4	1,505	+20.5	+71.6
Total	$67,488	$94,180	+39.6%	$125,316	+33.1%	+85.7%

Source: *Governmental Finances in 1975-1976*, U.S. Dept. of Commerce, Bureau of the Census, 1977 and *Governmental Finances in 1978-79*, U.S. Dept. of Commerce, Bureau of the Census, 1980.

State and local governments allocated $82.3 million of their 1973-1974 revenue sharing entitlements to public libraries, with the bulk, or $76 million, allocated by counties and municipalities and the balance by state governments. Of the $76 million, about 40% went to capital improvements, helping to fill a void created by the elimination of funding for LSCA II beginning in 1973. However, the $76 million of local shared revenue allocated to public libraries in 1973-1974 was a minute portion, 1.8%, of total shared funds, again indicating that libraries do not get high priority in competition for local funds.

Moreover, figures for 1977 peg combined state and local revenue sharing funds going to libraries at $79.7 million, or only 1.2%. Legislation providing for revenue sharing has been renewed and altered in the 1980s so that state revenue sharing funds will have to be appropriated each year. While local revenue sharing funds will still operate more or less as an entitlement program during 1982, funds may be cut as part of the Reagan administration's budget paring moves.

Analyzing early revenue sharing data, the National Commission on Libraries and Information Science (NCLIS) concluded that "no more than one-third to one-half of the $76 million allocated by municipalities and counties to public libraries resulted in increased library expenditure."[5] Although in many places revenue sharing funds undoubtedly resulted in avoidance of service cutbacks and allowed for acquisition of new facilities without borrowing at high interest rates, the report says: "The reality is that the great majority of local libraries have not participated in the revenue sharing largesse" and the great majority of municipalities and counties have not allocated a portion of their shared revenue to libraries.

On a broader plane, the NCLIS report concludes that federal funding efforts under LSCA and the general revenue sharing program "have been only moderately effective in assuring public library services." It urges a concerted nationwide effort to increase state fiscal support for the public library in closer conformity with state public education aid systems, and to expand utilization of public library services as an integral part of lifelong learning and expanded learning opportunities for both adults and children.

State Funds

Just as states provide different levels of financing for schools, there is wide variation in state fiscal capacity and effort in support of libraries. In 1980, 46 states provided some form of state aid to public libraries. On

THE SHRINKING LIBRARY DOLLAR

Table 2.21: Federal Funding for Major Library Programs, Fiscal Years 1977-1981

	1977	1978	1979	1980	1981	Reagan Proposal 1982	% Change 1977-1981	Proposed % Change 1977-1982
			(millions)					
ESEA IV-B (school libraries)	$154.3	$167.6	$180.0	$171.0	$171.0	$128.25	+ 10.8%	− 16.9%
LSCA I (Library services)	49.2	56.9	62.5	62.5	62.5	46.8	+ 27.0	− 4.9
II (Public)	0	0	0	0	0	0	0	0
III (Interlibrary cooperation)	3.3	3.3	5.0	5.0	12.0	12.0	+263.6	+263.6
National Library of Medicine	27.2	28.8	32.4	34.0	34.9	38.8	+ 28.3	+ 42.6
NCLIS	.5	.6	.7	.7	.7	.7	+ 40.0	+ 40.0
HEA II-A College libraries	10.0	10.0	10.0	4.9	4.9	0	− 51.0	
II-B Training	2.0	2.0	2.0	.7	.7	.7	− 65.0	− 65.0
II-B Demonstrations	1.0	1.0	1.0	.3	.5	.5	− 50.0	− 50.0
II-C Research libraries	0	6.0	6.0	6.0	6.0	6.0		

Source: U.S. Department of Education.

a national basis, the 1980 average per capita state aid for libraries was $.82. Figures compiled by the Urban Libraries Council indicate that a total of $166.5 million was appropriated for all purposes of state aid to public libraries, or $12.3 million more than 1979; and that these funds represented approximately 13% of the total amount expended for public library service in the U.S. By contrast, state funds accounted for 43% of funding for public elementary and secondary public schools.

The variation in library aid is extreme, ranging from $.03 in Ohio to $3.61 in West Virginia. In addition to West Virginia, Georgia ($2.47), Maryland ($1.98), New York ($1.78), Illinois ($1.62) and Pennsylvania ($1.49) contributed more than $1 per capita in 1980: other states topping the dollar mark are South Dakota ($1.26), Massachusetts and North Carolina (both $1.22), Rhode Island ($1.17), New Jersey ($1.14) and North Dakota ($1.05).

SUMMARY

There are approximately 104,000 libraries in the United States. Traditionally, these institutions are grouped into four major categories: public, academic, special and school. To these should be added federal, or government, libraries, a smaller but nonetheless important category.

Americans are generally pleased with the manner in which their public libraries serve them, according to a 1978 poll conducted by the Gallup Organization. Respondents were, however, unsure about the source of support for public libraries.

Growth in the number of librarians followed growth in library facilities between 1960 and 1970, but slowed down thereafter. Most rapid growth has been among public and special librarians.

There were 70,956 public library service outlets in fall 1978, of which 49,343 are bookmobile and mobile outlets, according to a major government survey. They offered services to nearly 200 million people.

In general, public libraries spend just over half their budgets on salaries and wages, with supplies and materials the next largest category. By far the largest portion of public library materials acquisitions is for books, which account for close to 80% of the total.

The large urban and suburban library systems, those serving populations of 500,000 and over, constitute the most important segment of the public library market. However, there are great variations in the resources offered by public libraries serving these and non-metropolitan populations.

Gaps in staffing, collections and expenditures are facts of life for public libraries, which have generally not kept up with needs in any of

THE SHRINKING LIBRARY DOLLAR

these areas, according to the *National Inventory of Library Needs—1975*. The report recommends huge increases in library funding, but does not suggest where the money might be found.

There are roughly 3000 academic libraries in the United States, including university, college, junior college and graduate level institutions. The Harvard University library ranked first in total number of volumes in 1976-1977, but the University of Texas (Austin) library spent the most on materials.

Academic libraries grew rapidly in the early 1970s, along with enrollments. Collections grew substantially, as did the number of periodicals and total library staff. However professional staff decreased in the latter part of the 1970s.

Rising costs continue to erode the capabilities of academic libraries to build collections and provide services. The expected trend in academic libraries to shift materials expenditures from book to periodical purchases did not occur.

Total materials acquisitions by academic libraries are expected to rise substantially between 1976 and 1984, going from $386.3 million to $680.1 million, a gain of 76%. The increase reflects price inflation, not unit growth.

There were 70,854 school libraries in the United States, according to a 1978 government survey, which said these institutions served 40.6 million pupils, down 7.5% from 1974.

The school library market became depressed in the mid-1970s, when a number of factors mitigating against acquisitions of books and audiovisual materials came together. These include declining enrollments, tight school budgets, consolidation of facilities, taxpayers' resistance to education costs, lower federal funding and higher teacher salaries.

The forecast for school library purchases between 1976 and 1984 was bleak especially for audiovisual materials, with purchases expected to fall by 15%. While expenditures on books and periodicals are expected to rise considerably, a good part of the increase will be due to price inflation since the number of periodical units is actually forecast to decrease 5%. Book units are predicted to rise an estimated 31%.

Statistics on special libraries are not profuse, but there were an estimated 15,000 special libraries in the United States in 1980.

Acquisitions of materials by special libraries are expected to rise to $710.1 million in 1984, with periodical acquisitions showing the largest dollar gains but book acquisitions reflecting a larger gain in unit purchases.

Overview of Libraries in the U.S.

There were 2142 federal libraries in the United States at the time of a 1978 government survey, including three national libraries and 2139 other federal libraries.

Though states are playing an increasingly important role in library funding, localities still provide nearly three-quarters of public library funds. Revenue sharing funds have been helpful to libraries, although these institutions do not get high priority in competition for local funds. Moreover, revenue sharing funds may dry up significantly in the early 1980s.

FOOTNOTES

1. Data from *Public Libraries, 1977-78,* U.S. Department of Education, National Center for Education Statistics (unpublished).
2. Data from *Public Libraries, 1977-78,* U.S. Department of Education, National Center for Education Statistics (unpublished).
3. *Indices of American Public Library Circulation and Expenditures,* Library Research Center, Library School, University of Illinois. Two indices are involved, one for expenditures, one for circulation. A new random sample of public libraries is chosen at the start of each decade, and the annual indices are computed for that sample.
4. It should be pointed out that figures on number of academic libraries differ depending on which source is used, e.g., *The American Library Directory* or U.S. government figures. Therefore, composite figures are being used in this report.
5. National Commission on Libraries and Information Science, *Evaluation of the Effectiveness of Federal Funding of Public Libraries.*

3

The Library Market for General Books

For the purpose of this discussion, general books include adult trade and juvenile books (hardcover and softcover), religious books and mass market paperbacks. In 1979, total publishers' sales of all these books were reported by the Association of American Publishers to be $1.99 billion, a 7.1% increase from $1.86 billion in 1978.

Based on estimates made by the Book Industry Study Group (BISG) and summarized in Table 3.1, an estimated $408.5 million was spent on general book acquisitions by U.S. libraries in 1979 and $446.0 million in 1980. This represented 56.0% of estimated dollar purchases of all domestically published books by libraries in 1979 and 56.0% in 1980, as well as 27.8% of total materials acquisitions by libraries in 1979 and 27.7% in 1980.

School libraries constitute the largest library market for general books, making acquisitions of $167.0 million in 1979 and $187.3 million in 1980. Expenditures for general books by school libraries are expected to rise to $247.2 million by 1984, 31.9% higher than the 1980 figure.

After school libraries, public libraries are the largest customer for general books. Sales to public libraries will rise 38.4% between 1980 and 1984 according to BISG projections.

Academic and special libraries, smaller customers for general books, will, nonetheless, increase purchases between 1980 and 1984, 51.6% for academic libraries (all trade books) and 40.2% for special libraries (trade and religious books).

These dollar expenditures will translate into moderate increases in unit sales in the overall adult trade category, where BISG forecast unit sales to increase 18.3% between 1978-1984 and only 15.7% between 1980-1984. Mass market paperback unit gains will show greater strength, up 22.8% between 1978 and 1984 and 25.4% between 1980 and 1984. Adult hardbound unit sales also show strength, up 24.5% in the six years between 1978 and 1984, and 22.5% between 1980 and 1984. In the juvenile category, unit sales of paperbound books, a small category, will

The Library Market for General Books

Table 3.1: Estimated Acquisitions by U.S. Libraries of Domestic Trade Books, 1978-1984

(millions)

	1978	1979	1980	1981	1982	1983	1984	% Change 1978-1984	% Change 1980-1984
Academic									
Trade	$65.7	$70.7	$78.0	$89.0	$100.4	$108.6	$118.3	80.0%	51.6%
Public									
Adult trade hardbound	65.1	64.4	66.8	75.6	80.6	87.1	94.7	45.5	41.8
Adult trade paperbound	14.1	15.1	15.8	16.8	18.0	20.1	21.9	55.3	38.6
Juvenile	46.9	46.5	49.2	52.6	56.5	59.2	63.5	35.4	29.1
Mass market paperback	9.5	10.8	10.6	11.2	12.9	14.6	17.0	78.9	57.4
	135.6	136.8	142.4	156.2	168.0	181.0	197.1	45.3	38.4
Special									
Trade	18.1	20.1	23.2	25.8	28.6	30.6	34.2	90.0	47.4
Religious	12.4	13.9	15.1	16.0	17.2	18.4	19.5	57.3	29.1
	30.5	34.0	38.3	41.8	45.8	49.0	53.7	76.0	40.2
School									
Adult trade hardbound	30.7	31.5	35.8	39.0	40.9	44.3	46.9	52.8	31.0
Adult trade paperbound	4.3	5.6	5.8	6.2	6.5	6.8	7.7	79.1	32.8
Juvenile	83.2	84.5	90.6	96.0	103.0	107.5	117.7	41.5	29.9
Mass market paperback	39.8	45.4	55.1	60.1	61.5	67.4	74.9	88.2	35.9
	158.0	167.0	187.3	201.3	211.9	226.0	247.2	56.4	31.9
Total	$389.8	$408.5	$446.0	$488.3	$526.1	$564.6	$616.3	58.1%	38.1%

Source: *Book Industry Trends, 1980*, Book Industry Study Group, Research Report No. 10, 1980.

outpace those of hardbound books. Religious book unit sales were forecast to rise an estimated 1.8% between 1978 and 1984; the predicted decrease between 1980 and 1984 is 0.8%.

THE ADULT TRADE BOOK MARKET

The rapid growth of the library market in the past two decades has without doubt contributed to the rise in total output of new titles and editions from 10,000 to about 40,000 annually. It is widely assumed that many titles would never be published if there were no library market to guarantee sales of a minimum number of copies. St. Martin's Press, for example, publishes small editions of many books annually which are virtually presold to the library market; although print runs do not number more than 3000 to 3500, it is confident of selling most of these copies. For most categories of books, the percentage of sales accounted for by libraries is inversely proportional to the total number of copies sold; that is, libraries account for a larger proportion of short run titles.

Library sales accounted for 13.8% of the total general book sales in 1980. Since mass market paperback sales to libraries are small, it is probable that trade sales to libraries as a percentage of all trade sales are closer to 22%, or more than one of every five trade books sold.

Because the hardcover trade book has become a relatively expensive item in recent years, many people look to libraries for the books they want to read. It has been estimated that 95% of the general titles published sell fewer than 20,000 copies, and an estimated 55% of the copies sold among these non-bestsellers go to libraries.

The library market for non-bestsellers is even more crucial because publishers earn a higher profit margin on library sales. There are several reasons for this. First, a significantly smaller percentage of sales is spent to advertise, promote and sell books to libraries than to bookstores, since a sizable field sales force is needed to build bookstore sales. Library sales, as discussed below, are more dependent on non-direct methods. Second, publishers do not have to bear the cost of returns from libraries. Third, because library sales are less quixotic than retail sales, the publishing risk is less and publishers are less likely to be left with overstocks of titles.

Table 3.2 which analyzes book publishing costs at alternative levels of production, indicates that editorial costs are not proportionally lower for short run books. Thus, publishers who feel that they have a market for perhaps 3000 or more copies in libraries will be guaranteed a better return on investment than those who publish a similar number of copies but do not anticipate "guaranteed" library market sales.

The Library Market for General Books

Table 3.2: Book Publishing Costs at Alternative Levels of Production

	Number of Copies		
	2000	5000	10,000
Fixed and Semi-Fixed			
Editorial and design	$ 3,500	$ 4,500	$ 6,000
Plant (composition and plates)	6,000	6,000	7,000
Overhead	5,000	5,500	5,500
Total fixed	14,500	16,000	18,500
Variable			
Printing, paper, binding	4,000	6,400	11,000
Promotion, warehousing, shipping	2,300	5,000	18,000
Royalty (based on 80% sold)[1] at $15@ list price	3,600	9,000	12,000
Total variable cost	9,900	20,400	41,000
Total cost	$24,400	$36,400	$59,500
Fixed costs as % of total	59	44	31
Cost/book printed	$12.20	$7.28	$5.95

[1]Royalty at 15% of list on those sold.
Source: Knowledge Industry Publications, Inc.

The best solution, of course, is a book which can be sold in both the library and trade markets. Based on the assumptions in Table 3.2, a book which generates 80% sales of 10,000 copies could gross some $69,600 for the publisher, based on a receipt of 58% of list price. The publisher would earn a comfortable profit of $11,100. If the book were ultimately to sell 40,000 or 45,000 copies in subsequent printings, the publisher could earn almost $140,000 pretax, as Table 3.3 illustrates.

Unit sales of adult trade books will grow 15.7% between 1980 and 1984. At the same time, dollar sales, fueled mainly by price increases, will rise 41.9%. Because of diminished funding (in constant dollars) in public libraries, which account for about 32% of all library purchases of adult trade books, no buoyant upturn is anticipated in unit sales, although dollar sales will continue to reflect publishers' price increases.

Table 3.4 gives the top 10 publishers of adult hardbound books, based on 1979 sales.

THE JUVENILE BOOK MARKET

After adult trade books, the second largest category of expenditures by libraries among general books is for juvenile books. Both public and school libraries are customers for juvenile books.

THE SHRINKING LIBRARY DOLLAR

Table 3.3: Profit and Loss Statement for a Trade Book Selling 40,000 Copies

Revenue ($8.70 net × 40,000)		$348,000
Expenses		
Fixed		18,500
Variable:		
Manufacturing	40,000	
Promotion, warehousing, etc.	60,000	
Royalties	90,000	
	190,000	
Total expense		208,500
Net income (before taxes)		$139,500

Source: Knowledge Industry Publications, Inc.

Total publishers' sales of juvenile books in 1979 were $185 million with the library market accounting for more than $130 million of that amount, or more than two-thirds of total volume. Many juvenile publishers derive the bulk of their sales from the library market: Scribner

Table 3.4: Leading Hardcover Publishers Based on 1979 Sales

Leading Hardcover Trade Publishers, 1979 vs. 1978

Rank	Company	1978 Sales (millions)	1979 Sales (millions)
1	Random House[1]	$80.0	$85.5
2	Harper & Row[2]	61.8	65.5
3	Simon & Schuster[1,4]	40.5	60.0 – 65.0
4	Doubleday[1,2]	50.0	55.0
5	Crown/Outlet[1]	40.0	45.0
6	Grosset & Dunlap[3]	59.0	35.0 – 38.0
7	Little, Brown[1]	22.0	24.0
	Putnam's[1]	22.0	24.0
8	Macmillan[1]	20.0	22.0
9	William Morrow[2]	18.5	20.0 +
10	Houghton Mifflin	17.1	15.9
11	St. Martin's	—	15.7

[1]Estimate.
[2]Fiscal year ended April 30, 1980.
[3]Fiscal year ended February 29, 1980.
[4]Fiscal year ended July 31, 1980.
Source: Knowledge Industry Publications estimates, publishers' annual reports and 10-K statements, and *Literary Market Place* (New York: R.R. Bowker, 1981).

The Library Market for General Books

Book Co.—80% to 90%, Parents' Magazine Press—85%, and Viking—60%.[1]

Because of the importance of the library market to publishers of juvenile books, the sales efforts of the juvenile or children's book divisions of many of these companies are concentrated almost exclusively on the institutional market. As with many trade titles, it is fair to assume that few juvenile books, except for the mass market-oriented titles published by companies like Western Publishing Co. (Golden Books) and Grosset & Dunlap, among others, would appear in print were it not for the library market.

Juvenile books sold to the library market are heavily dependent on reviews for sales. Since six months to a year may elapse before a juvenile book is reviewed, there may be a significant time lag between a book's publication date and when it begins to sell. This is balanced by the fact that juvenile books tend to sell over a longer time than many adult books.

In addition to reviews, book awards peculiar to the juvenile field, including the Newbery and Caldecott Medal and Honor Awards, are important for library sales. Most libraries purchase Medal or Honor books for their juvenile collections, and continue to replace them over the years.

Unfavorable demographics and the depressed state of library funding may keep juvenile book sales in the library market at sluggish levels in the years ahead. The high birth rate of the 1950s and 1960s has given way to a slower rate of childbearing, and birth expectations of women of childbearing age in the U.S. have remained at low levels, with 2113 children per 1000 women expected by those most likely to give birth according to the mid-1978 Census Bureau population report.

In the area of library funding, public and school libraries, the two primary buyers of juvenile books, have been hardest hit by library funding problems. Nevertheless, unit sales of juvenile books are expected to rise 20% between 1979 and 1984.

THE MASS MARKET PAPERBACK MARKET

During the 1960s and 1970s, mass market paperbacks found their way into many public and school libraries as well as into school classrooms through the aggressive efforts of certain publishers and wholesalers. In 1958, R.R. Bowker Co. estimated that libraries spent $2.5 million on paperbacks, which represented a scant 2% of all mass market publisher sales. The Book Industry Study Group estimates that in 1979-1980 school libraries spent $55.1 million on mass market paperbacks and public libraries more than $10.6 million, bringing total expenditures by libraries

THE SHRINKING LIBRARY DOLLAR

on books in this category to nearly $66 million, 9.2% of 1980 mass market sales.

Most of the mass market paperbacks sold to libraries are reprints of titles originally published by hardcover publishers, although an increasingly larger number of paperback originals are being issued, and subsequently finding their way into libraries.

Mass market paperbacks are sold to libraries in basically the same way as other books, direct by the publisher and through library wholesalers. In addition, local independent distributors (IDs), who deal in paperbacks and magazines, may sell mass market titles to libraries, although they generally find this unprofitable because of the low number of copies per title purchased by libraries. Those who do sell to libraries try to provide assortments of titles in high enough quantities to generate sufficient sales volume.

The mass market paperback field is highly concentrated, with the top eight publishers accounting for 74% of 1979 sales and the market leader, Bantam, generating 14% of 1979 paperback sales. Other leading publishers are Dell, CBS (including Fawcett, Popular Library), New American Library, Ballantine, Pocket Books, Avon and Warner.

Price Increases of General Books

A substantial portion of the revenue increases generated by general books in the 1970s and early 1980s has come from price increases. In the hardcover area, adult trade books posted the largest increase, more than doubling in price. In 1969, for example, the average price of a hardcover book on the *New York Times* bestseller list ranged from $4.95 to $5.95. In December 1978, the average price of the top five fiction bestsellers on the *New York Times* list was $12.67, with the range going from $9.95 to $15.00. The average price of the top five nonfiction bestsellers was $13.27, based on a range of $7.95 to $17.50. Table 3.5 illustrates selected 1980 prices. In December 1980, the average price was $14.16, with the range going from $12.95 to $15.95.

In the mass market paperback area, fiction titles increased 120.0% in price, going from $.17 to $1.65 from 1969 to 1978 and another 89.7% from 1978 to 1980. The average is now $3.13 and many of the biggest selling titles, such as *Smiley's People* (Bantam, $3.50), *Triple* (New American Library/Signet, $3.50) and *The Establishment* (Dell, $3.25) now bear prices above $3.13. Juvenile titles, which had already increased 98.6% in price from 1969 to 1978, religious titles, up 103.5%, and sports and recreation, up 109.2%, all broke the $2.50 barrier and were approaching a $3.15 average, in the case of juveniles, and the $4.50 and $6.00 mark in the other two categories, respectively, in 1979.

The Library Market for General Books

Table 3.5: List Prices of Selected Hardcover Fiction and Nonfiction Trade Books, 1980

	List Price
Fiction	
The Covenant (Random House)	$15.95
The Key To Rebecca (Morrow)	12.95
Unfinished Tales (Houghton Mifflin)	15.00
Firestarter (Viking)	13.95
Come Pour The Wine (Arbor House)	12.95
Average Price	$14.16
Nonfiction	
Cosmos (Random House)	$19.95
Crisis Investing (Stratford Press/Harper)	12.50
Side Effects (Random House)	8.95
Peter The Great (Knopf)	17.95
Goodbye Darkness (Little, Brown)	14.95
Average Price	$14.86

Source: Knowledge Industry Publications, Inc. based on *New York Times Book Review*, Dec. 28, 1980.

CHANNELS OF DISTRIBUTION FOR TRADE BOOKS

Libraries can either purchase books directly from the publisher or order through a library jobber. (The term jobber is generally used interchangeably with wholesaler). In the case of mass market paperbacks, purchase may be from an independent distributor.

Although bookstores may order multiple copies of certain books, particularly those of bestseller or potential bestseller status, librarians generally need only one or two copies of any title. However, they must offer their patrons a greater variety of books than the average bookstore. Since publishers do not want to be bothered fulfilling the small orders required by thousands of librarians, a happy solution for both publisher and library is for the library jobber to act as a middleman.

Jobbers who concentrate on the library market, such as Baker & Taylor, which calls itself the Librarian's Library, and Brodart, which dubs itself The Library Company, are essentially involved in a service business, ordering and processing the books libraries want from publishers. In addition, they may by involved in getting back orders and providing a variety of services, including cataloging.

An added advantage for libraries is that they often qualify for a higher discount by ordering through a jobber than by placing the order directly with a publisher. Library jobbers often offer discounts of 35% and 40%

THE SHRINKING LIBRARY DOLLAR

on trade titles vs. the 10% to 35% discount allowed by publishers directly on small orders.

More than two thirds of library acquisitions are made through library jobbers, with trade books more likely to be acquired through jobbers than other, more specialized books. School libraries rely most heavily on jobbers, followed by public, academic and finally special libraries.

According to the Book Industry Study Group, in 1980 an estimated 72% of all trade sales to libraries were made through wholesalers. This accounted for $131.8 million in sales. The balance, or 28%, of trade sales to libraries were direct sales from the publisher to the library, accounting for $51.4 million in sales. The percentage of sales to libraries through wholesalers range from a high of 75% for adult trade hardbound books to a low of 55% for religious trade titles.

Many libraries buy general books almost exclusively from a single wholesaler, based on a contract award through competitive bidding. The quality of service offered is often given higher priority than lowest discount in determining the successful bidder. In addition, libraries look for wholesalers who can supply the highest percentage of titles ordered in the shortest time period and with the fewest mistakes.

HOW PUBLISHERS REACH THE LIBRARY MARKET

Although publishers may distribute their books to libraries through wholesalers or jobbers, they still must promote their titles to these institutions. The most common publisher strategies for generating library sales include having books reviewed in the appropriate publications, advertising in appropriate publications, exhibits at library conferences, catalogs and brochures addressed to librarians, and promotion of a variety of standing orders or approval plans.

A 1974 survey sponsored by a joint committee of the Association of American Publishers and the American Library Association assigned the following rankings to methods of informing libraries of publishers' books:

Most Effective
Reviews
Publicity

Least Effective
Advertising
Flyers

Blanket order plans offered by
wholesalers and publishers
Catalogs
Exhibits
Visits by salespeople

Librarians' decisions to purchase particular titles are made on the basis of a number of factors, ranked by the AAP/ALA survey: favorable reviews, coverage of a subject area not previously represented, literary quality, important new work on a well-covered subject, inclusion on a recommended booklist, authority of the author.

Conversely, factors ranked less important by librarians in the AAP/ALA survey included personal knowledge of a book through reading it, requests by patrons, bargain price, information obtained at conference exhibits, contact by salesperson.

The Importance of Book Reviews

It is clear from the findings of the AAP/ALA survey that it is extremely important that general books be reviewed in the right places in order to maximize sales to librarians. Table 3.6 lists book review media and number of reviews in 1978 and 1979. Some of these media confine their reviews to a single type of literature, such as *Library Journal,* which reviews only adult titles, and *Horn Book,* which limits itself to juvenile and young adult titles. In general, there is a dearth of reviews of young adult titles, an amorphous category which could include many titles reviewed as "adult" books.

It is estimated that fewer than 10% of all books published annually in the United States are reviewed. In general, however, the number of book reviews has increased in the late 1970s, with Table 3.6 showing that most review media listed, except *Booklist* and *New York Times Sunday Book Review,* increased the number of reviews in 1979 over 1977.

Booklist, Choice, and *Library Journal* accounted for the largest number of reviews in both 1977-1979, each with approximately 5500-6800 reviews. Of these three review media, only *Booklist* reviews juvenile and young adult books.

Breaking reviews into three categories: adult, juvenile and young adult, *Choice* carried the most adult reviews in 1977, over 6700, followed by *Library Journal,* 6000. In the juvenile area, *School Library Journal,* with over 1000 reviews, was the leader, followed by *Booklist,* over 1400, and *Kirkus Service,* 1250. In the young adult area, in which only four review media are active *(Booklist, Bulletin of the Center for Children's Books, Horn Book* and *School Library Journal),* all review media with the exception of *Horn Book* accounted for more than 300 reviews.

R.R. Bowker's *Bookviews* stopped publication after the December 1978 issue. *Bookviews* had a short life span, publishing just 16 issues following its launch in September 1977.

In addition to these book review media, many large libraries have systems of reviewing books for themselves, using selection or review committees. Bulletins are usually issued to members of these library systems giving recommendations made by the committee.

Retrospective Book Purchases by Libraries

About 75% of the general books bought by libraries are titles acquired for the first time. The remaining 25% are backlist titles purchased to replace worn or lost titles or to fill gaps in collections. For this retrospective purchasing, a different set of information becomes important in making selection decisions. Important selection tools for backlist titles include *Books in Print* (R.R. Bowker Co.), *Book Review Digest* and *Cumulative Book Index* (both Wilson), book dealer catalogs, the Library of Congress Catalog and subject bibliographies. Because of the importance of these selection tools, publishers wishing to maximize library sales need to get their titles listed in as many places as possible.

Table 3.6: Book Review Media, 1977 and 1979

Publication	Approx. No. of Reviews, 1977	Approx. No. of Reviews, 1979
Booklist	6800	5500
Bookviews	900	—
Bulletin of the Center for Children's Books	800	850
Choice	6700	6800
Horn Book	500	500
Kirkus Service	4100	4850
Library Journal	6000	6000
New York Review of Books	450	550
New York Times Sunday Book Review	2600	2300
Publishers Weekly	4500	4900
School Library Journal	2300	2500
West Coast Review of Books	1300	2600

Source: Knowledge Industry Publications, Inc.; *The Bowker Annual of Library and Book Trade Information,* R.R. Bowker, 1980.

Direct Sales to Libraries

Although many publishers to whom the library market is an important source of revenue eschew direct sales, a handful of publishers, including

The Library Market for General Books

Doubleday and Macmillan, do send their sales force to call on libraries to persuade librarians to order direct. Publishers of trade books made 7.1% of their sales directly to libraries. The percentage for juvenile hardbound was 6.4%. Based on total trade and religious book sales of $1017.1 million (which excludes mass market paperbacks) this would mean about $72.1 million in sales were made by publishers to libraries. Table 3.7 gives domestic net trade book sales by type of customer.

Among the companies which are heavily reliant on direct sales to libraries are Doubleday, Scribners and Macmillan. Doubleday, for example, offers a wide range of standing order programs and approval plans, including the Junior Literary Guild, Elementary School Plan, High School Plan and subscription programs for mysteries, science fiction, westerns and romantic suspense titles. It has some 40 salespeople who call on libraries, and derives 65% of its juvenile sales from the library market.

The argument can be made that the sales force does not add a significant amount to publishers' total sales to libraries but merely switches them from the wholesaler directly to the publisher. Even though the books are sold to libraries at a lower discount than they are sold to wholesalers, it is unlikely that the difference in discount is enough to cover the cost of fielding an institutional sales force to sell general books. In view of this, there seems little rationale for publishers to compete with wholesalers, who are, in effect, their largest customers, for library business.

LIBRARY WHOLESALERS

Library wholesalers include those that sell a wide range of books of all publishers either nationwide or in a wide regional area, or who confine their activities to specific categories of books or to particular geographic regions. The first group includes the giants of the library wholesaling business, Baker & Taylor and Brodart, while the latter includes smaller companies like Thames Book Co. (New London, CT) and the Thomas More Association (Chicago).

Library wholesalers work with the thin margins generally associated with such middlemen. There are a variety of reasons for this situation.

First, these companies are expected to supply services as well as a product, and competition is keen among their ranks as to who offers the best service. Services include quick fulfillment of a large number of titles, backordering out-of-stock titles, cataloging and processing. Improving the efficiency of these services is considered a key to improved profit margins in the library wholesaling business. In many cases the discount spread of what the wholesaler gets from publishers and what he gives to

THE SHRINKING LIBRARY DOLLAR

Table 3.7: Domestic Net Trade Book Sales by Type of Customer, 1979

Customer	1979 (millions)	% of Total
Bookstores	$529.4	52.0%
Wholesalers	356.7	35.1
Prebinders	3.0	.3
Libraries & Institutions	72.1	7.1
Mass Market Outlets	10.2	1.0
Special Sales	25.4	2.5
Direct to Consumer	20.3	2.0
Total	$1017.1	100%

Source: Association of American Publishers, *Industry Statistics, 1979.*

libraries is insufficient to cover the costs of the services demanded by libraries. This explains why book wholesaling is a "thin margin" business and why smaller companies have trouble turning a profit and, in fact, remaining viable.

Second, as already noted, library funding is barely keeping pace with inflation, and the dollars expended on materials purchases are buying less than they have in previous years. It is therefore becoming increasingly necessary for wholesalers to promote themselves aggressively, supplementing publishers' promotion with their own programs.

During the 1970s a number of major library jobbers went out of business or incurred serious financial problems. Among them were Campbell & Hall, whose assets were bought by Booksmith Distributing Co. in 1973, and Richard Abel, whose assets were aquired by Blackwell in early 1975. In addition, the H.R. Huntting Co., (Chicopee, MA), which filed a voluntary petition for rearrangement under Chapter XI in July 1978, was acquired by Brodart, which will operate it as the Huntting Division. Demco, once part of the George Banta Co., was purchased from that company by a group of executives and subsequently sold its hardcover book inventory to Baker & Taylor. Another wholesaler which emphasized the school market, Josten's, substantially reduced its direct sales force, which numbered just two at the end of 1978, and indicated it would rely on catalog and mail sales. In December 1978, Brodart acquired Dimondstein Book Co., Inc. and in March 1979, Brodart acquired Josten's Library Services, Inc.

Looking to the future, wholesalers must contend with another wrinkle in the tangled library funding picture, the impact of tax reform measures, such as Proposition 13 in California and Proposition 2½ in Massachusetts. Libraries throughout California were adversely affected by the passage of Proposition 13, with many responding by cutting hours of service and book budgets. Brodart was the first library wholesaler to illustrate the impact of Proposition 13 on its business, posting a 49% earnings decline for the first quarter of its 1979 fiscal year, a drop attributed to sagging business in the Golden State. While revenues rebounded in 1980, higher costs forced Brodart to slash some discounts early in 1981. Brodart chairman Arthur Brady noted that publishers' returns policies were having a major impact on business, but more so on the retail rather than the library end of the business.

The difficulties in the library market and the development of book processing technology for the library market can do double duty in the retail book market, so several library wholesalers have intensified their efforts in the latter area. Baker & Taylor, for example, which once focused on the library market to the virtual abandonment of the retail sector, has become an aggressive factor in retail wholesaling, and expects that retail sales will assume a larger proportion of its total sales. It is listed in Table 3.8 as the largest wholesaler. Brodart, number three, has adapted its Instant Response Ordering System (IROS), originally designed for libraries, for booksellers and now offers a 24-hour Book Express service for bookstores in the metropolitan New York area. (Ironically, Book Express, although designed for bookstores, has also been utilized by libraries, who obtain faster order fulfillment, but not other services, from it.)

Ingram, the wholesaler which is generally conceded to have the largest share of the retailing market, ranks second to Baker & Taylor on an overall basis, with 1980 revenues an estimated $110 million. Although its activities in the library market constitute a small portion of its business, it is an aggressive and innovative presence in the retail market.

It is likely that the library wholesaler market will become more concentrated in the 1980s. The fate of Demco and Huntting are just the most recent examples of this consolidation, as small, regional companies are acquired by larger companies and those with more capital behind them. In

Table 3.8: Leading Book Wholesalers, 1980

Company	Revenues (millions)	% of Sales to Library Market
Baker & Taylor	$215.0	N/A
Ingram	110.0	10
Brodart	75.8	90
Blackwell North America	26.0	99.5
Bookazine	22.0	60

Source: Knowledge Industry Publications, Inc., and annual reports.

THE SHRINKING LIBRARY DOLLAR

addition to a reduction in the number of wholesalers, the libraries may also begin to be charged extra for services which wholesalers now provide as part of their contract.

Baker & Taylor, a subsidiary of W. R. Grace, would seem to be well positioned to increase its market share, with both the addition of Demco's hardcover business and an infusion of capital from W.R. Grace expected to beef up its already strong operation. Brodart is diversifying into the bookstore field and has strengthened its library stake by addition of H.R. Huntting's library supply business; it should also survive in the market. These two companies would appear to be in the best position to acquire smaller, regional wholesalers which find that they can no longer go it alone.

SUMMARY

Total publishers' sales of general books, covering adult trade, juvenile, religious and mass market paperbacks, were $1.99 billion in 1979, 7.1% higher than in 1978.

An estimated $446.0 million was spent on general book acquisitions by U.S. libraries in 1980. This represented 56.0 % of library purchases of domestically published books in 1980, as well as 27.6% of total materials acquisitions by libraries.

School libraries constitute the largest library market for general books, followed by public libraries. Academic and special libraries are smaller customers for general books. All types of libraries are forecast to increase purchases of general books between 1978 and 1984.

The dollar sales will translate into modest increases in unit sales in the adult trade category. Mass market unit sales are predicted to show somewhat greater strength, while unit sales of juvenile hardbounds should outpace those of paperbound books.

Trade book sales to libraries represent about one of every five books sold. Libraries represent an especially strong market for non-bestsellers, where library sales yield a higher profit margin.

The library market is important for juvenile books, with about 70% of sales generated in that market. Many juvenile publishers derive the bulk of their sales from the library market, and sales efforts of juvenile or children's book divisions are often concentrated almost exclusively on the institutional market. Juvenile books sold to the library market are heavily dependent on reviews and book awards for sales.

Most of the mass market paperbacks sold to libraries are reprints of titles originally published by hardcover publishers. Independent distributors, in addition to publishers and wholesalers, sell mass market titles to libraries.

A substantial portion of the revenue increases generated by general books in the 1970s has come from price increases. Fiction books, for example, more than doubled in price between the average 1967-1969 price and 1977 figures. Mass market fiction titles rose 120% in price in this period and another 89.7% from 1978 to 1980.

Libraries can purchase books directly from the publisher or purchase them through a library jobber. Baker & Taylor and Brodart are the two largest jobbers concentrating on the library market.

More than two-thirds of library acquisitions are made through jobbers, with trade books more likely to be acquired through these middlemen than more specialized books. School libraries rely most heavily on jobbers, followed by public, academic and finally special libraries.

Publishers reach the library market through book reviews, advertising, exhibits at library conferences, catalogs and brochures and promotion of a variety of standing order or approval plans by which libraries receive books automatically.

Some companies are heavily reliant on direct sales to libraries, fielding sizable sales forces to this market. They include Doubleday, Scribner Book Co. and Macmillan.

Library wholesalers provide services as well as books to libraries, and competition is keen among them. Wholesaling is a narrow margin business and smaller companies have difficulty making a profit while matching the services of their larger competitors. The impact of tax reform measures such as Proposition 13 in California has intensified an already difficult market for these companies, as have the returns policies of publishers.

FOOTNOTES

1. Judith S. Duke, *Children's Books and Magazines: A Market Study* (White Plains, NY: Knowledge Industry Publications, Inc., 1979).

4
The Library Market for Professional and Reference Books

In addition to constituting an important market for general books, libraries represent a major market for professional and reference books. For the purposes of this chapter, this category also includes university press and subscription reference books (encyclopedias). An estimated $237.9 million in domestically published books in these categories were acquired by U.S. libraries in 1980, representing 29.9% of all acquisitions by libraries of domestically purchased books and 14.7% of all materials purchased by libraries.

In addition to U.S. professional books, libraries buy millions of dollars of imported professional books each year. In 1980, for example, the Book Industry Study Group (BISG) estimated that $82.5 million in imported books were acquired, about two-thirds by academic libraries, the major customer for professional books, and most of the balance by special libraries. A substantial percentage of those acquisitions is believed to be professional books.

As seen in the projections in Table 4.1, by 1984 library acquisitions of domestically published professional and reference books are expected to total $389.3 million, representing 33.5% of all acquisitions by libraries of domestically published books and 17.7% of all materials purchased by libraries.

Unit sales are expected to increase for professional books, although far less rapidly than dollar increases. Unit sales for both university press and subscription reference books will also increase between 1978 and 1984, with university press books showing a slightly larger rise; between 1980 and 1984, unit sales in subscription reference will show a more substantial increase than those of university press books.

Academic libraries purchased $85.5 million of these books in 1980, a figure which is projected to rise 68.2% to $143.8 million in 1984. Special libraries are the next largest library customer for professional/reference books, with purchases of $76.0 million in 1980 expected to increase to $137.2 million in 1984, an 80.5% gain, to almost equal the total purchases of academic libraries.

Table 4.1: Estimated Acquisitions Expenditures by U.S. Libraries for Domestically Published Professional and Reference Books, 1987-1984

	1978	1979	1980	1981	1982	1983	1984	% Change 1978-1984	% Change 1980-1984
				(millions)					
Academic									
Professional	$52.0	$54.0	$59.6	$68.4	$84.7	$93.4	$106.2	104.2%	78.2%
University press	14.1	16.1	18.4	19.9	21.8	23.6	26.0	84.4	41.3
Subscription reference	6.0	6.8	7.5	8.8	9.5	10.7	11.6	93.3	54.6
	72.1	76.9	85.5	97.1	116.0	127.7	143.8	99.4	68.2
Public									
Professional	24.2	25.2	23.9	24.8	23.8	25.9	30.3	25.2	27.6
Subscription reference	7.3	7.9	8.7	9.5	9.7	11.1	12.1	65.7	39.0
	31.5	33.1	32.6	34.3	33.5	37.0	42.4	34.6	30.6
Special									
Professional	61.0	67.0	76.0	87.1	108.0	118.5	137.2	124.9	80.5
School									
Professional	27.8	24.3	24.3	26.2	29.6	33.2	37.0	33.0	52.2
Subscription reference	16.0	17.6	19.5	21.2	23.2	25.8	28.9	80.6	48.2
	43.8	41.9	43.8	47.4	52.8	59.0	65.9	50.4	50.4
Total	$208.4	$218.9	$237.9	$265.9	$310.3	$342.2	$389.3	86.8%	63.6%

Source: *Book Industry Trends, 1980*, Book Industry Study Group, Research Report No. 10, 1980.

THE SHRINKING LIBRARY DOLLAR

Public and school libraries are smaller customers for professional and reference books. For public libraries, acquisitions of professional and reference books are expected to rise 30.6% between 1980 and 1984 while school library purchases will rise 50.4%

In general, the library market for professional and reference books can be expected to grow in the 1980s because the major library customers for these books are those that are less dependent on public funds and tax-inspired budget constraints. Another factor fueling the increase in library acquisitions of these books is the increasing trend toward continuing education in the United States, an area in which many professional and reference books can be used.

PROFESSIONAL BOOKS

Professional book sales alone totaled $885.1 million in 1979. Table 4.2 lists the types of books tabulated in this category. Almost 9% of professional books, or $75.2 million, are purchased directly by libraries with another 9%, or $79.7 million, purchased by library jobbers. This means that the final destination of close to 18% of all professional books in 1979 was libraries, lower than BISG estimates which indicate that $170.5 million in professional books were sold to libraries by publishers in 1979.

Special libraries are the largest customers for professional books, accounting for 39.3% of their sales to libraries, with academic libraries a close second with 31.7% in 1979, according to BISG. School libraries accounted for 14.3% of professional book sales to libraries and public libraries generated 14.8%. According to the Association of American Publishers (AAP), academic libraries are the largest customers, accounting for 38% of their sales to libraries. School libraries accounted for 19%, and public libraries generated 25.5%, with the remainder attributed to "other."

Technical and Scientific Books

Sales of technical and scientific books were $301.1 million in 1979, with about 79% of those sales domestic and the balance to foreign markets, led by Asia (5.8%), the United Kingdom (5.4%), and continental Europe (4.0%).

Included in this category for the purpose of this study are books for scientists, technicians and scholars that are intended as tools to aid them in their professions; monographs covering developments in specific areas; specialized reference works (including dictionaries, encyclopedias,

The Library Market for Professional and Reference Books

Table 4.2: Sales of Professional Books, 1979

	Sales (millions)	% of Total Category
Technical and scientific		
Math., probability, statistics	13.8	4.6
Computer sciences	19.0	6.3
Engineering	69.6	23.1
Biological sciences	25.3	8.4
Physical sciences	35.8	11.9
Earth sciences	8.7	2.9
Social sciences	69.6	23.1
Architecture	18.4	6.1
Other technical and scientific	40.9	13.6
	$301.1	100.0%
Business and other professional		
Business	122.8	33.2
Law	13.0	3.5
Education	45.9	12.4
Other business and professional	188.3	50.9
	$370.0	100.0%
Medical		
Medicine	112.6	52.6
All other medical	89.9	42.0
Not allocated	11.5	5.4
	$214.0	100.0%
Total, professional	$885.1	

Source: Association of American Publishers.

handbooks, abstracts and indexes), and reprints of out-of-print technical, scientific and scholarly works.

Typically these books are published for small groups of specialists rather than a large general audience. Thus, sales of many of these titles are often no more than 1000 to 2000 copies, with the great majority under 5000. Many are sold directly to libraries at discounts ranging from none to 30%.

Academic libraries and special libraries are expected to increase their acquisitions of technical and scientific books 99.4% and 124.9%, respectively, between 1980 and 1984. Projections for other libraries are in Table 4.1.

For the most part, titles bought by these libraries consist of advanced treatises, monographs, handbooks, symposia and series in science and applied science.

THE SHRINKING LIBRARY DOLLAR

There are close to 250 publishers of science, math and technology books who publish at least five titles per year. Leaders in this field include Academic Press (Harcourt Brace Jovanovich), Macmillan, John Wiley, McGraw-Hill, Prentice-Hall and Van Nostrand Reinhold.

Because of the low discounts on technical and scientific titles, a large proportion of sales to libraries is made directly by publishers. Direct mail is the most widely used means of reaching libraries, and a few publishers use a limited number of salespersons to call on libraries as well.

John Wiley & Sons, for example, relies entirely on mailings. The company has a publication for libraries listing every new title that Wiley publishes. Some university libraries, in turn, will order every Wiley title. The overall reputation of a scientific-technical publisher like Wiley is an important factor in getting academic libraries to purchase most or all of its titles.

Outside of standing order plans with various publishers, different members of the library staff are responsible for individual purchasing decisions on technical and scientific, and other professional, books. In larger libraries, a specialist in a given technical and scientific field, e.g., computer sciences or engineering, would provide input on titles in that field. In smaller libraries, the library director may be the one involved in a purchase decision. In all cases, however, the library users, especially faculty members and professional staff at academic and special libraries, have a great impact, in the form of requests channeled through the reference desk.

Scholarly Reprints

A 1971 study by Carol Nemeyer identified more than 300 reprinters. Nemeyer estimated that libraries spent about $12 million annually for such books.[1] Knowledge Industry Publications, Inc. estimates that annual sales in the early 1980s are closer to $25 million.

Academic libraries constitute the largest market for scholarly reprints, which got a big boost from the infusion of federal funds into the library market in the Great Society years of the 1960s.

Scholarly reprints are sold to libraries primarily by direct mail. Other sources of sales are wholesalers and salespeople. Publishers often announce their works in catalogs before printing scholarly reprints, in order to raise capital as well as to test the market.

Leading publishers of scholarly reprints include Johnson Reprint Co. (Harcourt Brace Jovanovich), with estimated 1980 sales of around $7 million, and Arno Press, which includes Benjamin Blom and Books for

The Library Market for Professional and Reference Books

Libraries (all New York Times Co.), with estimated revenues of around $6 million in 1980. Other publishers in the field include Kraus Reprint Co., Kennikat Press, AMS Press and Greenwood Press. These publishers may issue hundreds of titles a year (1100 in the case of Arno in 1980) or just a few.

Business and Other Professional Books

Library acquisitions of business and other professional books (see Table 4.2) are greater than their technical and scientific book purchases. In 1979, libraries accounted for 24.7%, or $91.4 million, of the $370.0 million in business and professional book sales. In addition, library jobbers accounted for an estimated $15.9 million in professional book sales.

Two types of libraries—public and academic—are major customers for business and other professional books, with special and school libraries understandably accounting for a smaller percentage of acquisitions.

As with technical and scientific books, publishers of business and other professional books rely heavily on direct mail, which is supplemented in some cases by direct sales and/or by wholesaler or jobber efforts. Books are sold either at full price or for a small discount.

Leading publishers of business and other professional books include Prentice-Hall, which had $45.6 million in professional book sales in 1979; McGraw-Hill; the American Management Association (AMACOM); Richard D. Irwin (Dow Jones); Dartnell; John Wiley & Sons; and Van Nostrand Reinhold.

In addition to business and professional books, libraries also spend millions of dollars annually on financial and business directories and looseleaf services published by a variety of companies, ranging from full-range publishers to specialists in this field.

Examples of materials in these areas include directories and looseleaf services (Prentice-Hall, Standard & Poor's, the Bureau of National Affairs, Commerce Clearing House, among others); hardcover directories which provide detailed reference information on companies and their managers (Dun & Bradstreet, Standard & Poor's); frequently updated looseleaf services covering financial subjects, federal legislation, regulations and court decisions affecting business (Dun & Bradstreet, Value Line Investment Services, Prentice-Hall, Bureau of National Affairs, Commerce Clearing House). Well known looseleaf services include *Federal Taxes Service* (Prentice-Hall) and *Common Market Reports* (Commerce Clearing House).

THE SHRINKING LIBRARY DOLLAR

Law Books

Sales of law books constitute only a small fraction of total business and professional book sales, according to AAP. A number of the major legal publishers, including West Publishing and Lawyers Coop, do not report their sales for the Association of American Publishers' Survey and must therefore be estimated. The market for law publications, however, is substantial, amounting to more than $200 million in 1978 and encompassing legal tests, legal dictionaries, court opinion reports, looseleaf reports, citations and a host of other legal publications. About 25% of law book sales go to libraries, the bulk of them to academic and special libraries.

Law books are almost always sold directly to libraries by publishers, with the key to library market sales resting in making an initial sale, since most titles are published in series.

The largest publisher in the law book publishing field is West Publishing (St. Paul, MN), which publishes *Black's Law Dictionary*, court opinion reports and other law books. Another leader in the law book field is Lawyers Coop (Rochester, NY), publisher of *American Jurisprudence* as well as other encyclopedias and *Supreme Court Reports*. Matthew Bender (New York, NY), part of Times Mirror Co., publishes about half of the major law textbooks, and was among the first to publish law texts in looseleaf form, to enable easy updating.

In addition, libraries purchase looseleaf services and legal periodicals. Commerce Clearing House is the leading publisher of looseleaf topical law reports on fields such as federal and state income tax, estate tax, federal and state labor legislation and general business law. Others include the Bureau of National Affairs (Washington, DC) and Prentice-Hall (Englewood Cliffs, NJ), which publish legal looseleaf services on subjects such as tax management, labor relations and business law.

Another specialist in the legal publishing field is Oceana Publications (Dobbs Ferry, NY), which publishes international law books and, through its Glanville Publishers subsidiary, bibliographic reference tools used by law libraries. The latter include *Law Books in Print, Law Books Published, Law Books in Review, Index to Periodical Articles Related to Law* and *Legal Periodicals in English*.

Medical Books

Publishers' sales of medical books are listed as a separate category within the overall professional book area by AAP, which reported medical sales of $214 million in 1979. Only about 8.5% of this total is to libraries, primarily those associated with medical schools, hospitals and research institutions.

Medical books are sold to libraries primarily through commissioned sales representatives and direct mail. Some specialized jobbers, such as Majors Scientific Books, also handle them. Non-library sales are made primarily to doctors or to students for use as textbooks. One estimate is that 36.3% of medical books were individual sales, the majority of them via direct mail.

As in the case of other professional books, most medical books are published in series and are sold to libraries via standing order and continuation plans. Leading publishers of medical books include W.B. Saunders (CBS), which published 100 titles (not all medical) in 1980 and has estimated annual medical revenues of around $48 million; C.V. Mosby (Times Mirror); McGraw-Hill; Williams & Wilkins (Waverly Press); J.B. Lippincott (Harper & Row); Lea & Febiger; Macmillan; and Yearbook Medical Publishers (Times Mirror). John Wiley & Sons, whose College Division and Wiley-Interscience medical titles were combined to form a new division, Wiley Medical, in 1973, is also involved in medical publishing.

The Role of Wholesalers in the Professional Book Market

Wholesalers active in selling professional books to libraries include Baker & Taylor, Ballen, Blackwell North America, Brodart, Coutts and Midwest Library Service. Baker & Taylor, for example, stocks more than 30,000 scholarly titles and has some 200 "approval" customers in the U.S. among academic libraries, to whom new titles are shipped automatically with full return privileges.

The number of wholesalers serving academic libraries is small, numbering perhaps eight or 10 who are viable, only a handful of them operating on a national basis. As a result, the market is highly concentrated.

Baker & Taylor, for example, offers approval programs under which libraries receive automatic, weekly shipments of all newly published books deemed to be of interest to specific institutions. Essential elements of the approval program include a profile of each individual library's requirements, Baker & Taylor's professional book selection and a computer match of new titles to the library's profile.

A library can make its profile even more specific by choosing modifiers, such as publisher, place of publication, price limit, academic level, physical format, etc. The profile of each new approval program title is computer matched with individual libraries' profiles: when a match occurs, an order is placed for the title. (Chapter 6, The Library Market for Systems, discusses additional services offered by wholesalers in the library market.) The plethora of services offered by wholesalers is expensive to maintain. Substantial growth for these companies will occur mostly by taking market share from one another, while profits depend on finding ways to continue to offer libraries the services they expect at lower costs.

An estimated 57.5% of professional book acquisitions in 1980 were made through wholesalers, the balance direct from publishers, and this percentage is expected to remain essentially constant through 1984.

Price Increases of Professional Books

While the decade since the late 1960s had been one of substantial overall growth for publishers of professional books, it has also been one of soaring average prices. In general, prices of professional and reference books almost doubled in this period, the impact being the slower growth of units as compared to dollar purchases of these titles by libraries.

According to figures from the Book Industry Study Group, the average unit prices of professional books acquired by special libraries rose from $14.47 in 1975 to $21.54 in 1979, an increase of 49%.

Professional books sold to academic libraries rose from an average unit price of $14.49 in 1975 to $21.09 in 1979, an increase of 45.5%. The average price of subscription reference materials, on the other hand, rose at a comparatively lower rate, from $365 in 1975 to $493 in 1979, an increase of 35.1%.

Rapidly escalating prices in the professional/reference book field also spilled over to paperback business books, which rose from $5.10 in 1967-1969 to $6.91 in 1977 and paperback science books, up from $4.06 to $8.83, in this period. By 1980, business paperbacks had risen to $10.14 and science paperbacks to $12.76.

UNIVERSITY PRESS BOOKS

University press books, which, according to AAP figures, generated $68.0 million in total sales in 1979, also find a large market in libraries, especially academic libraries. University press acquisitions by libraries represented close to one-third of sales or $24.2 million in 1980, and have been increasing about $3.0 million annually in recent years.

The Library Market for Professional and Reference Books

Dollar sales of university press titles to libraries have continued to grow; here too, copy sales are gaining. Libraries are expected to buy only 2.34 million copies of these titles in 1983-1984, compared to 2.13 million copies in 1979-1980. This represents almost a 10% increase in unit sales over that period, with dollar sales ahead 37% over that same span.

Financial pressures on universities to reduce subsidies to their own presses has made it difficult for some presses to survive on a sound financial basis, and has led to publication of fewer titles.

SUBSCRIPTION REFERENCE BOOKS

Sales of subscription reference books (encyclopedias) were $415.0 million in 1980, with less than 4% or about $17.4 million of this coming from library sales. Academic libraries are the major library customers for subscription reference books, followed by school, public and special libraries.

Sales of subscription reference books were up 35.0% between 1975 and 1978, rising from $252.7 million to $341.2 million. They increased in 1980 to $415.0 million.

In addition, there has been considerable change among several of the major encyclopedia publishers. Grolier, Inc. incurred serious financial difficulties beginning in 1974, because of irregularities at its Americana Interstate subsidiary and foreign exchange losses, while Field Enterprises sold its World Book—Childcraft subsidiary to Scott & Fetzer in mid-1978.

The four largest publishers of subscription reference books—Encyclopaedia Britannica (EB), Grolier, Field, Macmillan—account for about 90% of industry sales and an even larger share of sales to libraries. EB publishes the 30-volume *Britannica 3,* which sells to libraries for $699 per set. In addition, it publishes *Compton's Encyclopedia, Great Books of the Western World* and *Annals of Americanis,* a 19-volume collection of American history. Grolier publishes the 20-volume *New Book of Knowledge,* aimed at school age children, as well as the *Encyclopedia Americana* and the *Encyclopedia International.* Field publishes the *World Book Encyclopedia* and also *Childcraft—The How and Why Library,* while Macmillan's subscription reference titles include *Collier's Encyclopedia* and the *Merit Student's Encyclopedia.*

Encyclopedias are sold to libraries through both a sales force and direct mail. Grolier, for example, claims to have more than 100 salespeople calling on this market.

Specialized Encyclopedias

In addition to the encyclopedias already mentioned a number of other companies, including McGraw-Hill, John Wiley & Sons and Van Nostrand Reinhold have a large stake in the specialized encyclopedia market. Examples of these include Wiley's *Kirk-Othmer Encyclopedia of Chemical Technology,* which will include 24 volumes when completed and is promoted as "the Bible of the chemical field," and the McGraw-Hill *Encyclopedia of Science and Technology,* a 15-volume work.

Despite the sluggish state of the U.S. encyclopedia market and stagnant library budgets, sales of specialized encyclopedias have done well in the late 1970s and prospects are for modest growth. Those in the field claim that while libraries can do without many acquisitions when budgets are tight, encyclopedias, (especially those involved with current technology), are mandatory.

Furthermore, editions appear less frequently than with other books (one every six years or so), thus increasing demand on another front. One specialized encyclopedia publisher expressed confidence about the market, based on the hypothesis that if you have a good product and it finds a niche, librarians, who are "there for service," will buy it.

Direct mail accounts for a major proportion of specialized enclyclopedia business, which is also characterized by lower than average returns and strong demand in export markets. On the other hand, publishers undertaking specialized encyclopedia projects must be well financed, because of high fixed and upfront expenses.

OUTLOOK FOR PROFESSIONAL AND REFERENCE BOOK SALES TO LIBRARIES

The market for professional and reference books has been growing. Professional book sales as a total category rose 132.3% between 1972 and 1979, outpacing more than half of all AAP categories.

This growth took place despite the recession in the mid-1970s, which was generally felt to reduce research and development budgets for a period of time.

A number of factors augur well for growth of this product in general in the 1980s, and for library acquisitions in particular. First, a shift in social priorities is creating new demands for published materials in fields such as urban affairs, energy requirements, environmental protection

The Library Market for Professional and Reference Books

and related areas. Second, economic problems, including those associated with inflation, are also creating new demands for publications in this area. Third, there is the pronounced trend toward continuing education, including advanced professional education and continuing self-development, creating new markets for materials once limited to the few.

In all these areas, libraries are in the forefront in answering public demand for such publications, as the information explosion in the U.S. creates a demand for a reservoir of all types of professional and reference books.

SUMMARY

Libraries spent an estimated $237.9 million on domestically published professional and reference, university press and subscription reference books in 1980, representing 29.9% of all acquisitions by libraries of domestically purchased books and 14.7% of all materials purchased by libraries.

In addition to U.S. professional books, libraries buy millions of dollars of imported professional books each year.

Library acquisitions of professional and reference books are growing, and are expected to total $389.3 million by 1984, or 33.5% of all acquisitions by libraries of domestically published books and 17.7% of all materials purchased by libraries.

Academic libraries, the major market for professional and reference books, purchased $85.5 million of these books in 1980, and are expected to purchase $143.8 million in 1984. Special libraries, the next largest customer, spent $76.0 million on professional and reference books in 1980, a figure which is expected to increase to $137.2 million in 1984.

Almost 18% of all professional books sold in 1979 were to libraries.

Sales of technical and scientific books were $301.1 million in 1979. Academic and special libraries are expected to increase their acquisitions of technical and scientific books 99.4% and 124.9% respectively between 1980 and 1984.

Sales on a large proportion of technical and scientific titles are made directly by publishers, with direct mail the most widely used means of reaching libraries.

A 1971 study on the scholarly reprint market identified more than 300 such publishers. Estimated sales of scholarly reprints in 1980 were $25 million, with academic libraries constituting the largest market for such titles.

Libraries acquired $91.4 million in business and professional books in

THE SHRINKING LIBRARY DOLLAR

1979. Two types of libraries—public and academic—are the major customers for these books, which are sold heavily by direct mail. Materials in this area include directories and looseleaf services.

The market for law publications amounted to over $200 million in 1978. Law books are almost always sold directly to libraries. Since most titles are published in series, the key to library market sales rests in making the initial sale. In addition to books, libraries purchase looseleaf services and legal periodicals.

Medical book sales were estimated to be $214 million in 1979, with only about 8.5% of this amount generated by libraries. Medical books are sold to libraries primarily through commissioned sales representatives and by direct mail. Like legal books, many medical books are published in series.

Wholesalers active in selling professional books to libraries include Baker & Taylor, Ballen, Blackwell North America, Brodart, Coutts and Midwest Library service. These wholesalers offer approval programs and various other plans for purchase of professional books, and an estimated 57.5% of professional book acquisitions in 1980 were made through wholesalers.

In general, prices of professional and reference books almost doubled between 1975 and 1979, with professional/reference paperbacks also feeling substantial price increases.

University press books sold an estimated $24.2 million in libraries, mainly academic institutions, in 1980. Unit sales of these titles have increased also.

Sales of subscription reference books were $415 million in 1980, with less than 4% of this total coming from libraries. Academic libraries are the major library customers for subscription reference books, which are sold both direct and through direct mail.

The outlook for professional and reference book sales in libraries is buoyant, as libraries strive to answer the demand for publications dealing with shifting social priorities, such as urban affairs, energy requirements, environmental protection, tax matters, inflation and the like.

FOOTNOTES

1. Carol Nemeyer, *Scholarly Reprint Publishing* (New York: R.R. Bowker Co., 1972).

5

The Library Market for Periodicals

In 1980, public, special and school libraries in the United States spent an estimated $436.6 million on periodicals, or 28.7% of total expenditures for materials. More than half this sum, or $243.2 million, was spent by special libraries, and 93%, or $404.2 million, was spent by academic and special libraries.

For purposes of this study, the term "periodical" will be defined as any publication issued in parts with a numerical or chronological designation, issued more frequently than once a year on a regular basis or over an indefinite period of time. Included in this definition are magazines, newspapers, journals, government publications and indexing and abstracting services. Not included are monographic series, yearbooks, annual directories and similar regular or irregular serial publications.

Table 5.1 gives estimated library acquisitions of periodicals, broken down by type of library, for even years, 1976 through 1984. It shows that periodicals are forecast to be a growing percentage of library acquisitions, rising from 25.8% of total acquisitions in 1976 to 28.1% in 1984. Periodical acquisitions by academic, public and special libraries will all increase between 1976 and 1984 as well as between 1980 and 1984. Special libraries and public libraries show the greatest increase and academic libraries the least.

Overall, periodical purchases by libraries are forecast to rise 111.2%, outpacing overall materials acquisition growth, forecast to be up 93.4% in this period. Growth between 1980 and 1984 is expected to be slower for periodicals, up 33.8%, and will not outpace total materials acquisitions, projected to rise 36.6%.

Growth in periodical acquisitions was projected to be more rapid in the 1976 to 1980 period than between 1980 and 1984.

The fact that academic and special libraries account for almost 93% of total library expenditures for periodicals indicates that more money is spent for scholarly and research periodical literature than for general interest consumer magazines.

THE SHRINKING LIBRARY DOLLAR

Table 5.1: Estimated Library Market for Periodicals, Even Years, 1976-1984

	1976	1978	1980	1982 (millions)	1984	% Change 1976-1984	% Change 1980-1984
Academic Libraries	$ 131.5	$ 145.6	$ 161.0	$ 182.2	$ 203.7	54.9%	26.5%
Public Libraries	16.2	19.8	24.8	30.7	39.5	143.8	59.3
Special Libraries	118.4	173.3	243.2	288.1	332.4	180.7	36.7
School Libraries	27.6	30.5	34.6	39.2	44.8	62.3	29.5
	$ 293.7	$ 369.2	$ 463.6	$ 540.2	$ 620.4	111.2%	33.8%
Total library acquisitions	$1139.9	$1377.2	$1613.2	$1895.7	$2204.1	93.4%	36.6%
Periodicals as % of total library acquisitions	25.8%	26.8%	28.7%	28.5%	28.1%		

Source: *Book Industry Trends* 1980, Book Industry Study Group, Research Report No. 10.

THE MAGAZINE INDUSTRY

Total revenue of the U.S. periodical publishing industry in 1980 was $8.9 billion. As figures in Table 5.2 show, these revenues have grown 126% since 1975. Government projections indicate that they will increase by another 11% in 1981.

The trend for an increasing proportion of total revenue to come from circulation revenue—despite record advertising revenues—may be leveling off. This means that subscription price increases have outpaced advertising increases. Scholarly journals have, of course, had to meet almost all their higher costs from subscriber payments.

In 1980, $3.7 billion in circulation revenue was achieved by in excess of 3000 companies and not-for-profit organizations which distributed more than 6 billion copies of their publications. These range from Time Inc. with magazine sales of $747 million to tiny professional societies that publish single journals with circulations of only a few hundred copies.

Library expenditures do not equal receipts by publishers because most of these sales go through subscription agents. Knowledge Industry Publications estimates than an average of 88% of the money spent by libraries reaches the publisher with the remaining held by agents as commissions and fees.

Any given library does not have to deal with the universe of some 60,000 periodicals published. In fact, American Library Association standards call for small public libraries to maintain subscriptions to only 75 to 150 magazines, and for senior high school libraries to have 125 to 175 subscriptions. For the most part, these titles consist of the 180 magazines indexed in *Reader's Guide to Periodical Literature* (H.W. Wilson). An adequate collection for junior colleges and colleges is considered to be 400 to 1000 titles. These are not particularly large numbers, especially when compared to the total of over 4500 magazine titles reviewed in *Magazines for Libraries* (R.R. Bowker Co., 3rd ed., 1978), which the compilers think should be considered by public, college and school libraries. The large university and public research libraries and some special libraries, on the other hand, may subscribe to as many as 5000 or more titles.

How Periodicals are Sold to Libraries

About 77% of the periodicals purchased by libraries are bought through agencies and 95% of all libraries use these agents, who act as middlemen between publishers and libraries. Libraries send their orders for periodicals to one or more of these agents who group them by

THE SHRINKING LIBRARY DOLLAR

Table 5.2: Periodical Publishing Revenue and Percentage from Advertising and Circulation, 1975-1981

Percent from:	1975	1976	1977	1978	1979	1980	1981
Advertising revenue	56.6%	54.5%	53.8%	53.7%	54.2%	53.6%	NA
Circulation revenue	43.4	45.5	46.2	46.3	45.8	46.4	NA
Total	100.0%	100.0%	100.0%	100.0%	100.0%	100.0%	
Total product value (billions)	$3.773	$4.455	$5.528	$6.518	$7.343	$8.151	$9.047
Total revenue (billions)	$4.379	$5.043	$6.056	$7.160	$8.052	$8.937	$9.920

NA: Not available
Source: U.S. Dept. of Commerce, *U.S. Industrial Outlook, 1981*

The Library Market for Periodicals

publisher before forwarding them. Consumer magazine publishers usually give agents large enough discounts to permit them in turn to offer libraries subscriptions at small discounts over regular prices. In cases in which publishers allow only small discounts or no discounts at all, agents must charge libraries fees for servicing subscriptions.

The two largest catalog subscription agents are Ebsco Subscription Services (Birmingham, AL) and F.W. Faxon (Westwood, MA). These two firms offer libraries a worldwide list of 150,000 and 100,000 titles, respectively. In addition to magazines, these titles include newspapers, annuals, irregular and less than annual series, proceedings and transactions, monographic series, book series, government documents, etc. Ebsco, in particular, considers research and identification of hard to locate titles an important part of its services.

Very few agents handle reprints or back issues, which must be either obtained directly from publishers or from dealers who specialize in back issues, out-of-print materials, reprints, etc. A leading dealer in back issues is Abrahams Magazine Service, Inc. of New York City. This firm advertises that it has 400,000 periodical and serial titles available. To obtain titles requested by libraries, these firms publish "want lists" which are distributed to other dealers and collectors.

Agents range in size from Ebsco and Faxon downward to one-person field agent operations which can handle only 60 to 100 of the mass circulation magazines for a group of libraries. In between are small to medium-size agents who have access to most American titles required by the small to medium-size library.

Among the larger agents is Moore-Cottrell Subscription Agencies, a company which purchased Maxwell International Subscription Agency. Both of these firms make more than 60,000 titles available to libraries. Maxwell is particularly strong in scientific and technical publications.

Stechert-Macmillan, a division of Macmillan, Inc., serves all types of libraries and provides more than 40,000 titles. The McGregor Magazine Agency, which specializes in magazines and makes more than 6000 titles available, says its list includes all magazine titles, both American and foreign, which can be ordered through agents.

Many libraries use one or more international subscription agents in addition to domestic agents. Leading companies in this field include Blackwell North America, Stevens & Brown and Swets and Zeitlinger.

Subscription agents batch library orders and send the publishers one order for many libraries. They also make advance payments to publishers which saves the publishers the time and expense of billing. Publishers allow agents discounts ranging from 0 to 50%, with the average being 9%.

THE SHRINKING LIBRARY DOLLAR

In recent years, many publishers have been either reducing or entirely eliminating these discounts and agents in turn are adding service charges to libraries for handling subscriptions in order to compensate for the lower discount. These fees usually are around 10% of the cost of the subscriptions.

Most agents send libraries annual review lists of their subscriptions to be used in compiling the coming year's orders. These lists include the original list of subscriptions plus new items and cancellations in addition to the latest prices and the expiration dates of subscriptions if they are not ordered on a "til-forbid" basis.

Agents are strongly opposed to making bids for library business and will do so, if at all, reluctantly and selectively. They claim that the time and expense involved are prohibitive and that it is difficult to meet certain performance and service criteria. However, it is reasonable for a library to ask for quotes when a library is contemplating hiring or changing an agent. Quotes differ from bids in that they simply require providing list prices of available titles and a schedule of the charges for needed services.

The Importance of Library Subscriptions

The importance of sales to libraries to the more than 2500 U.S. periodical publishers varies widely depending upon the type of periodical. On an industry-wide basis the $436.6 million spent by libraries is 12.0% of the circulation revenue of American publishers. Library subscriptions of many mass circulation magazines are insignificant to the publishers. Publishers of controlled circulation trade magazines (those sent for free to audiences qualified by the nature of their jobs and the magazine's subject matter) often refuse library subscriptions because of the need to restrict circulation to potential customers of the advertisers.

On the other hand, library sales can be of crucial importance to many general interest "quality" magazines that have literary, social, political, economic or scientific relevance and small circulations. Subscriptions for libraries, which usually come in through catalog agents, often account for 10% or more of the circulation revenue of these publications. Libraries are a major and in many cases the largest source of circulation revenue for publishers of scholarly and research journals, particularly the thousands of titles with circulations below 3000 copies. It can be safely generalized that for serious periodicals, the importance of library sales is inversely proportional to the size of the circulation. Libraries form a basic core market without which many publications would not be able to exist.

The Library Market for Consumer Magazines

Most of the magazines in public and school libraries are consumer magazines and these are concentrated among those indexed in *Reader's Guide to Periodical Literature*. These 180 magazines represent 12% of the 1500 consumer magazines listed in the *Standard Rate and Data Service*.

Table 5.3 lists six of the largest consumer magazines found in most public, school and college libraries along with the average paid circulations of these magazines as of the last six months of 1980.

Special interest consumer magazines for which library sales are significant include publications of literary, political, economic, social and scientific importance. Some of the most important of these magazines, listed in Table 5.4, are *Smithsonian, Business Week* and *Scientific American*.

Table 5.3: Leading Mass Circulation Magazines of Interest to Libraries, 1980

Name of Magazine	Publisher	Paid Circulation
Reader's Digest	Reader's Digest Assn. Inc.	17,898,681
National Geographic	National Geographic Society	10,711,886
Time	Time Inc.	4,358,911
Newsweek	Newsweek, Inc.	2,964,279
Sports Illustrated	Time Inc.	2,265,760
U.S. News & World Report	U.S. News & World Report, Inc.	2,055,993

Source: *Standard Rate and Data Service*, from Audit Bureau of Circulation Statements, June 30, 1980 to December 31, 1980.

Table 5.4: Leading Special Interest Magazines of Importance to Libraries, 1980

Name of Magazine	Publisher	Paid Circulation
Smithsonian	Smithsonian Institution National Associates	1,904,515
Business Week	McGraw-Hill Publications Co.	824,259
Scientific American	Scientific American, Inc.	712,902
Saturday Review	Saturday Review Magazine, Corp.	511,101
New Yorker	The New Yorker Magazine Co.	503,124
The Atlantic	The Atlantic Monthly Co.	332,004
Harper's	Harper's Magazine Co.	361,438

Source: *Standard Rate and Data Service*, from Audit Bureau of Circulation Statements, June 30, 1980 to December 31, 1980.

THE SHRINKING LIBRARY DOLLAR

Prices of Consumer Magazines

The average cover price of the 297 consumer magazines audited by Audit Bureau of Circulation increased from $.39 in 1960 to $.63 in 1970, to $1.03 in 1977 and to $1.33 in 1979. The increase since 1970 has been 111%. The higher prices which libraries must pay for consumer magazines are resulting in a shift of funds from books to magazines. The books to periodicals expenditure ratio in public libraries has shifted from 9.7 to 1 to 7.9 to 1 between 1976 and 1980 alone.

The Library Market for Scholarly and Research Journals

According to Bill Katz, editor of *Magazines for Libraries,* there are more than 40,000 scientific and technical journals published throughout the world. These journals have been proliferating in numbers in recent years and, as a result, are becoming increasingly specialized.

Bernard M. Fry, Dean of the Graduate Library School, Indiana University, has compiled a list of 2552 journals distributed by 1672 publishers for which library sales comprise a significant percentage of circulation revenue.

Two separate surveys of these publications resulted in a comprehensive economic description of the journal publishing industry in the United States.[1]

The figures in Table 5.5 show that most scholarly and research journals are published by 768 not-for-profit professional societies. These organizations account for 46% of the publishers in the sample and 43% of the journals. The 297 commercial publishers represent only 18% of the publishers but account for 26% of the journals.

Leading publishers of scholarly and research journals include the American Institute of Physics among the professional societies,

Table 5.5: Scholarly and Research Journals, 1977

Type of Publisher	Number of Publishers	Number of Journals	% Journals
Commercial (for profit)	297	670	26.3%
Professional Society	768	1099	43.1
University Presses	43	129	5.0
Other Not-for-Profit	564	654	25.6
Total	1672	2552	100.0

Source: *Survey of Publisher Practice,* National Commission on New Technological Uses of Copyrighted Works, 1977.

Table 5.6: Leading Publishers of Scholarly and Research Journals

Publisher	Subject Areas	No. of Journals 1977-78	No. of Journals 1980-81
Academic Press (Harcourt Brace Jovanovich)	Scientific & Technical	139	145
American Chemical Society	Chemistry	22	22
American Institute of Physics	Physics	47	64
American Medical Association	Medical	20	15
Marcel Dekker, Inc.	Scientific & Technical	43	56
Johns Hopkins University Press	Social Sciences, Medical	9	15
MIT Press	Scientific & Technical	6	14
Pergamon Press	Scientific & Technical	226	375-400
Plenum Publishing Corp.	Scientific & Technical, Russian	135	148
Sage Publications, Inc.	Social Sciences	45	48
M.E. Sharpe, Inc.	Social Sciences, Russian Translations	27	30
University of California Press	Social Sciences, Humanities	8	11
University of Chicago Press	Social Sciences, Humanities	37	40
John Wiley & Sons	Scientific & Technical	25	24
Williams & Wilkins Co. (Waverly Press)	Medical	30	79
		819	1119-1144

Source: Knowledge Industry Publications, Inc.

THE SHRINKING LIBRARY DOLLAR

Pergamon Press and Academic Press among English-language commercial publishers, and University of Chicago Press in the university press category. Others are identified in Table 5.6.

The mean circulation of the core list of journals is 8906. However, more than 50% of the journals (65% of commercial journals) have circulations less than 3000 copies, while only one-fifth have as many as 10,000 subscribers. These breakdowns by size of circulation are shown in Table 5.7.

Table 5.8 shows that in the five year period from 1972 to 1977, the average journal increased its circulation 21.5% or 4% a year compounded. However, the circulation of commercial publishers increased 40.0% while not-for-profit journals increased by only 15.8%. Journals in the field of applied sciences showed the largest increase in circulation, 28.4%, compared to journals in the pure sciences, which were the slowest growing, 9.5% annually.

Price Increases of Journals

While circulations of journals have been growing at modest rates, prices have been rising at a faster clip. In 1977, the average price of a one year subscription to an American periodical was $24.59, 9.2% higher than the average price of $22.52 in 1976. By 1978, the average price of 3255 titles had risen to $27.58, another 12.2% increase. Since 1970, subscription prices have been increasing at an annual compound rate of 13.0%. By 1980, the average price of 22,768 titles had risen to $69.35, a 151.5% increase. Looking at a few specific categories, the average price of chemistry and physics journals has risen 643.9% from 1970 to 1980, home economics 420.1% and law, 271.3%.

In general, sci/tech journal prices have been increasing faster than journal prices as a whole; chemistry and physics journals have traditionally been the most expensive and denominational and sectarian magazines the least costly. The 19 averages were $248.82 for chemistry/physics to $14.09 for denominational and sectarian magazines. Table 5.9 compares the three groups of journals. Natural science journals tend to be the highest priced, while literature, the arts and social sciences are among the least costly.

Economics of Journal Publishing

Whereas resource sharing has alleviated some libraries' financial problems, it has had a deleterious effect on publishers of scientific/technical

The Library Market for Periodicals

Table 5.7: Circulation Categories of Scholarly and Research Journals

Number of Copies	% Commercial	% Not-for-Profit	% of Total
Under 3000	64.8%	44.7%	50.5%
3000-9999	17.3	35.2	30.0
10,000 and over	17.9	20.1	19.5
	100.0%	100.0%	100.0%
Mean Circulation	8349	9135	8906

Source: *Survey of Publisher Practice,* National Commission on New Technological Uses of Copyrighted Works, 1977.

Table 5.8: Average Increase in Journal Circulation by Category, 1972-1977

Type of Journal	Number of Journals	Mean Circulation 1977	Percentage Circulation Increase 1972-1977	Annual Compound Growth Rate
Pure science	437	5,818	9.5%	1.8%
Applied science	785	12,935	28.4	5.1
Social science	986	8,839	20.9	3.9
Humanities	344	5,866	16.6	3.1
Commercial	—	8,349	40.0	7.0
Not-for-profit	—	9,135	15.8	3.0
Total	2,552	8,906	21.5%	4.0%

Source: *Survey of Publisher Practice,* National Commission on New Technological Uses of Copyrighted Works, 1977.

journals, who derive their income basically from subscriptions and have an inherently limited market because of their specialized subject matter. Some publishers had hoped that the new copyright law and the introduction of mechanisms such as the Copyright Clearance Center (CCC), discussed in Chapter 1, would help hard-pressed sci/tech publishers by providing fees for photocopying of their journals. However, CCC's initial year transaction volume was well below anticipated levels. While on the rise since, from $57,000 in 1978 to $243,000 in 1979 and $300,000 in 1980, CCC royalty collections still afford little economic relief to journal publishers who must keep up with an ever-expanding body of scientific information.

THE SHRINKING LIBRARY DOLLAR

Table 5.9: Comparison of Journal Prices, 1978-80

Subject	1978 Average 1 Year Price	1979 Average 1 Year Price	1980 Average 1 Year Price	% Increase 1978-1980
Group I ($45 and up)				
Chemistry & Physics	$177.14	$196.62	$248.82	+40.5%
Medicine	50.89	58.90	70.38	+38.3
Mathematics, Botany, Geology, General Science	65.70	74.07	89.40	+36.1
Engineering	77.29	90.70	100.76	+30.4
Zoology	49.79	57.89	73.05	+46.7
Psychology	45.96	51.36	57.21	+24.5
Group II ($22 and up)				
Home Economics	30.46	32.89	39.32	+29.1
Sociology-general	25.98	31.00	33.49	+28.9
Biblio, Lib. Sci.	30.46	32.89	39.32	+29.1
Law	27.80	33.26	36.54	+31.4
Poly Sci-Pol. Doc.	29.23	32.48	34.48	+18.0
Fine Arts & Visual Arts	22.99	25.64	26.48	+15.5
Group III ($11.00 and up)				
History-Amer. gen'l.	13.91	15.79	14.63	+ 5.2
Denomination & Sect.	11.11	13.64	14.09	+26.8
Lit. Hist. & Coll.-gen'l.	15.89	18.09	17.89	+12.6
Recreation	12.33	14.04	16.65	+35.0
Literature of Music	17.85	20.83	16.05	−10.6
Philology & Ling.	17.25	19.67	19.88	+15.2

Source: F.W. Faxon

Impact of Rising Prices

The increase in journal prices had a great impact on academic libraries, which increased expenditures for periodicals at the expense of the budget for books in the late 1970s but have reversed that trend in the early 1980s. Special libraries now account for more than half of all library expenditures for periodicals and academic libraries for about one third (see Table 5.1). However, as Table 5.10 shows, 77% of the 2750 academic libraries held fewer than 1000 periodical titles when the Fry report was done.

Table 5.10: Number of Periodicals Held by Academic Libraries

Number of Periodical Titles	Number of Academic Libraries	Cumulative Percentage
1 - 199	536	19.5%
200 - 499	952	54.1
500 - 999	639	77.3
1000 - 1999	277	87.4
2000 - 4999	205	94.9
5000 +	141	100.0

Source: Bernard Fry and Herbert S. White, *Publishers and Libraries: The Study of Scholarly and Research Journals*, (Lexington, MA: D.C. Heath/Lexington Books, 1976).

The largest 5% of the academic libraries or the 141 large university research libraries are the most important customers for the very specialized scholarly and research journals. Association of Research Libraries members, for example, spent $98.9 million on periodicals in 1979-1980.

There was a clear trend in the 1970s for academic libraries to increase their purchases of periodicals at the expense of books. This trend is not expected to continue in the 1980s. Table 5.11 shows that periodicals are forecast to decrease from 34.0% to 30.0% of academic library acquisitions between 1976 and 1984. Books, meanwhile, are forecast to increase from 52.1% to 59.4%

Prices of periodicals acquired by academic libraries are expected to rise rapidly in this period, from $42.01 in 1976 to $93.01 in 1984 on a unit basis, a 121% increase. Prices of books purchased by academic libraries are forecast to rise from $8.97 to $15.12 in this same period, a 69% increase. Academic libraries which were tending to dip into funds once used to buy books to maintain periodical collections as periodical prices rise seem to have reversed the trend.

Library Reaction to Rising Journal Costs

Journal subscription prices have been rising rapidly at a time when libraries have been faced with budget crises of their own. There are, however, several ways libraries can cope with higher periodical prices.

First, as has already been documented, they can allocate more of their budgets to periodicals, less to books. Ultimately, however, this will result in gaps in book collections.

Second, they can turn to resource sharing, in which case they do not have to order all the journals their patrons require provided they belong to a cooperative arrangement through which the required titles can be obtained. An example of such a cooperative venture is the Research Libraries Group, comprised of 23 owner/members including the New York Public Library and such universities as Yale, Stanford, Columbia, Michigan, Pennsylvania, Princeton, Dartmouth, Iowa, Rutgers, Brigham Young, Colorado State, Brown, Cornell, Johns Hopkins, NYU, Northwestern, Tulane, Minnesota, Temple, Oklahoma and Penn State.

Third, libraries can loan photocopies of requested journals, rather than originals, retaining the latter as a master copy to photocopy as needed. Although this alternative obviates the need for multiple subscriptions, it also means that someone else must bear the cost of obtaining the copy; in addition, it also raises questions of "fair use" under the copyright law.

There is no question that photocopying activities involving periodicals have proliferated, as documented by several studies. One, based on a 1974 Special Libraries Association survey and reported in the May/June 1976 issue of *Special Libraries,* cited periodicals as the most frequently copied material. Eighty-three percent of respondents had one or more copying machines in the library. It is likely that this trend has continued, and probably intensified, since the survey was taken. Another study, an original survey of photocopying by Knowledge Industry Publications,[2] reported that 71% of the respondents claimed that periodicals are more heavily copied than any other type of published materials. In addition, the survey revealed that periodicals of scientific/technical interest are more heavily copied than those of general interest by most libraries, when responses from four types of libraries were combined.

Also in 1977, the long-awaited study of library photocopying carried out by King Research (Rockville,MD) indicated that an estimated 114 million serial articles were copied on library photocopiers in 1976, and that a large majority of all photocopying subject to fee is done by a small percentage of libraries.

Proposal for a National Periodicals Center

A September 1978 plan published by the Council of Library Resources (CLR), proposed a National Periodicals Center (NPC) which would improve access to periodical literature for libraries and thus to patrons using libraries. CLR, in a 272-page document entitled "A National

Periodicals Center Technical Development Plan," proposed a national structure which would contain a centralized collection of periodical literature directly accessible to libraries throughout the U.S. The NPC was initially projected to hold 36,000 titles, with its collection envisioned as growing prospectively by adding more titles and retrospectively by acquiring back files. The collection would eventually number in excess of 60,000 current titles but never contain all of the estimated 200,000 published periodicals.

CLR said the NPC would be expensive, eventually paid for by a combination of federal subsidy and user fees, with a budget of $3.8 million the first year, $4.9 million the second year and $4.5 million the third year. Beyond the fourth year, in which CLR projected a basic operating expense of $1.9 million, costs would become more directly related to level of fulfillment activity. CLR set cost of a new building to house the NPC at between $5.5 million and $6.5 million.

The plan met considerable resistance in the library community as soon as it was announced. Eventually, a watered down proposal was included in the extension of the Higher Education Act calling for establishment of a nonprofit corporation to assess "the feasibility and advisability of a national system" rather than a national "center." However, the law required a certain amount of funding to trigger such action and Congress did not supply the necessary amount. Thus even the assessment of the feasibility of such a system remains in limbo.

SUMMARY

Libraries spent an estimated $436.6 million on periodicals in 1980. This represents about 30% of total expenditures for materials in 1980.

More than half of all expenditures for periodicals are made by special libraries. Together, academic and special libraries account for almost 93% of all periodical purchases by libraries.

Periodicals represent a growing percentage of library acquisitions, rising from 25.8% of total acquisitions in 1976 to an estimated 28.1% by 1984. Special libraries and public libraries show the greatest increase and academic libraries the least.

Periodical acquisitions are forecast to outpace overall materials acquisition growth in libraries between 1976 and 1984, rising 111.2% vs. 93.4% for all materials.

Total revenue for the U.S. periodical publishing industry was $8.9 billion in 1980. Government projections call for growth of 11% in 1981.

Periodicals are generally purchased by libraries through subscription agencies, with about 77% of periodicals reaching libraries by this means. The two largest subscription agencies are Ebsco Subscription Services and F.W. Faxon. Most agents send libraries annual review lists of their subscriptions to be used by libraries in compiling orders for the coming year.

Public and school libraries are most likely to buy consumer magazines, while academic and special libraries purchase scientific and technical journals and other scholarly publications.

Prices for both consumer and scholarly periodicals rose rapidly in the 1970s, resulting in a shift of funds from books to magazines by libraries anxious to maintain their periodical subscriptions. This shift is expected to show signs of abating in the early 1980s.

Most scholarly and research journals are published by not-for-profit professional societies, with commercial publishers representing less than 20% of such publishers. Leading publishers of scholarly and research journals include the American Institute of Physics (a professional society), Pergamon Press (a commercial publisher) and the University of Chicago Press (a university press).

Circulation of scholarly journals tends to be small. More than 50% of the journals cited in a 1977 study had circulations of under 3000 copies per issue.

Circulations of scholarly journals have been growing at modest rates, but price increases have been rising faster. Since 1970, subscription prices have been rising at an annual compound rate of 13%. In general, sci/tech journal prices have been increasing faster than journal prices as a whole.

Publishers of scientific/technical journals have been adversly affected by resource sharing, because they derive their income basically from subscriptions and have an inherently limited market due to their specialized subject matter.

Libraries have reacted to rising journal prices by allocating higher percentages of their acquisition budgets to periodicals, and correspondingly lower amounts to books. They have also turned to resource sharing, forming cooperative ventures such as the Research Libraries Group (RLG). In addition, libraries can loan photocopies of requested journals, rather than originals, retaining the latter as a master copy to photocopy as needed.

A National Periodicals Center has been proposed that would be intended to improve access to periodical literature for libraries and thus for patrons of libraries. However, lack of congressional funding has caused even a feasibility study of a periodicals system to languish.

FOOTNOTES

1. For further imformation see Bernard Fry and Herbert S. White, *Publishers and Libraries: The Study of Scholarly and Research Journals* (Lexington, MA: D.C. Heath/Lexington Books, 1976) and *Survey of Publisher Practice and Present Attitudes on Authorized Journal Article Copying and Licensing* (National Commission on New Technological Uses of Copyrighted Works, 1977).

2. Patricia Whitestone, *Photocopying in Libraries: The Librarians Speak* (White Plains, NY: Knowledge Industry Publications, Inc., 1977).

6
The Library Market for Systems

Just as the little red schoolhouse is a remnant of the past, replaced by sprawling elementary and secondary education complexes with media centers, physical education facilities and various multi-purpose rooms, the image of the traditional library, with its manual circulation procedure and grey-haired librarians overseeing the entire operation is passing from the scene. Libraries at the end of the 1970s and early 1980s are turning more and more to networks and technology to help them cope with an information explosion on the one hand and a budget crunch on the other. Their problem, essentially, is keeping up with the huge flood of information, manifested by the 35,000 to 40,000 books published in the U.S. alone each year as well as the soaring volume of scientific and technical information, estimated to double every 15 years, without any appreciable increase, and in some cases decreases, in the percentage of their budgets which goes for materials.

These two circumstances—increase in information and static budgets—have been an impetus for growth of resource sharing networks, consortia and related ventures. They have also prompted libraries to turn to computer technology to effect cost savings and streamline operations. Included here are computerized cataloging and processing services, online bibliographic services and other data bases and automation of other services, such as circulation systems and theft prevention. The result has been a burgeoning market for automated services and equipment, estimated at $134.5 million in 1981. Unlike materials budgets, which previous chapters have shown to be static or declining, this segment of the library market is vital and growing.

This chapter deals with the development of library networks, which facilitate resource sharing of all kinds, and the market for automated services and equipment in libraries.

LIBRARY NETWORKS

Libraries generally form networks to facilitate sharing of bibliographic information and collections and to provide better service for patrons. Networks can be online, using computers and linking members via telecommunications connections, or they can provide bibliographic data on a batch basis.

Although the growth of library networks is basically a phenomenon of the 1960s and 1970s, a loosely structured library network began to form over a century ago with the founding of the American Library Association and the increasing national activities of the Library of Congress (LC). Growth of networking accelerated when the Library of Congress led the way in the design of a format for machine-readable bibliographic records. The Library of Congress' five-year effort resulted in national, then international acceptance of the Machine-Readable Cataloging (MARC) format. Two years after distribution of the first machine-readable cataloging by LC, the Ohio College Library Center, now the Online Computer Library Center, Inc. (OCLC), began operations as the first online computer network for libraries.

By 1980, at least 22 computer-based library networks were in existence in North America, up from 18 in 1976. These ranged from a network of five academic libraries in upstate New York (Five Associated University Libraries), to huge regional networks such as the New England Library Information Network (NELINET) and Southeastern Library Network (SOLINET).

There are a number of types of library networks, including those providing technical processing on reference data bases. Networks can include all types of libraries. The Washington Library Network (WLN) has 21 public, 39 academic, 3 state, 1 special library and 1 regional center as members. Others are more restricted, such as the Capital Consortium Network (CAPCON), which consists of some 35 academic and specialized research institutions in the Washington, DC area. Organization of these networks varies, with control exerted by libraries, information centers, consortia of institutions of higher education and, in a few cases, commercial firms.

Many library functions are adaptable to a shared network processing, including cataloging new titles, acquisitions and interlibrary loans. On the other hand, other library functions, such as circulation, serials check-in and fiscal accounting, do not lend themselves as readily to shared network processing.

Since regional and other types of library networks have proven feasible, attention has been given to whether a nationwide network can be developed. Such a prospect may be a development in the future. At the end of 1980 a nationwide network was still the subject of discussion but it appeared that the concept had been overtaken by events. Each library and each network continued to hold its own priorities, "fitting into the national jigsaw as appropriate."[1]

ONLINE BIBLIOGRAPHIC SERVICES AND OTHER DATA BASES

Academic and special libraries and, in some cases, public libraries provide both online bibliographic data base services and other data bases to their patrons. Ryan E. Hoover, in *The Library and Information Manager's Guide to Online Services,* writes that "any library that regards itself as a vital information center for its patrons must use online services to support and augment its other information activities."[2]

Between 1975 and 1978, the number of machine-readable data bases more than tripled, growing from slightly more than 100 in 1975, fewer than half of which were online, to more than 360 in early 1978. By 1979 there were some 528 publicly available bibliographic data bases, a 46.7% increase. Originally most of these were in the scientific disciplines, but the number of data bases in the humanities, social sciences, business and general information has been growing. A number of factors fueled the growth of computer-based bibliographic services in this brief time span, chief among which, according to Hoover was "the mushrooming growth of scientific and technical information" and the steep increase in the cost of acquiring that literature. Further growth for bibliographic data bases, particularly those which are online, is projected because both the proliferation and the cost trends continue.

Various other factors also favor machine-readable bibliographic data bases. These include:

- The switch to photocomposition and other computer-aided production techniques on the part of publishers of conventional abstracting and indexing services;

- Technological progress in computer programming, storage, terminals and communications;

- Dramatic decreases in the cost of the necessary equipment;

- The declassification of government documents containing vital technical information;

- The increased acceptance by libraries of electromechanical equipment;

The Library Market for Systems

- The speed, comprehensiveness, currentness and cost-effectiveness of online information retrieval as opposed to manual searching of printed sources;

- The availability of sophisticated commercial services to provide nationwide access to various individual data bases.

The industry includes two main segments which are based on the different ways customers gain access to the computerized data base. One is the "batch mode" of operation, in which the customer writes or phones a data base supplier, who then returns the information requested by mail or by phone. Many different requests are "batched" for a single computer search. In addition, a customer may subscribe to an on-going service of computer-searched reports which are tailored to his specification, a type of service called Selective Dissemination of Information (SDI). Batch searching is not interactive and is done on data base tapes rather than discs. The tapes are searched sequentially from end to end.

The second mode of operation is the online method, in which a customer—or a librarian or trained searcher—dials the data base supplier's central computer from his own terminal, requests the information he needs and receives the data via a printer or visual display terminal (VDT) within minutes.

The batch mode segment of the data base business is large and mature, dominated by big old-line companies like the Institute for Scientific Information (ISI), Bio Sciences Information Service and Chemical Abstracts, which supply data base tapes to libraries and research laboratories for searching. The online segment, on the other hand, is a youthful industry, but is growing quickly. It includes Lockheed's Dialog Information Service and System Development Corp. in addition to the New York Times, Mead Data Central, Dow Jones and others. Moreover, more and more operations are being converted to the online mode and companies such as ISI and Chemical Abstracts are beginning to supply direct online access to data bases rather than through an online vendor.

Data bases are of two basic types, bibliographic and numeric. Bibliographic data bases are comprised of abstracts and titles of articles from scientific journals, research reports and the like. They are widely used by library patrons who desire a report of article abstracts or titles, the text of which can then be obtained from a library if more data are required. Numeric data bases consist of statistical information on many different economic and business matters. Some of these are manipulable, meaning they can be used to perform special correlations, analyses and forecasts.

A third type of data base is the full text base, as in certain legal files

THE SHRINKING LIBRARY DOLLAR

where every word of a court decision is stored in the computer.

Data base producers include The New York Times Information Bank, Chemical Abstracts Service (CAS), Engineering Index, the Institute for Scientific Information, the National Institute of Education, the Congressional Information Service, Dow Jones News Retrieval Service and many others.

Along with producers, there are online vendors, or distributors, of data bases. The five major search services—Bibliographic Retrieval Services (BRS), The New York Times Information Bank (NYTIB), Lockheed Information Systems, the National Library of Medicine and System Development Corp. (SDC)—offered more than 250 data bases at the end of 1980. Lockheed is the largest, identified in Table 6.1 as having 120 different data bases.

Data bases cover a wide variety of subjects. The New York Times Information Bank (NYTIB), much used by special libraries and government agencies, claims to offer the largest data base of general information abstracts accessible in English, based on material that has appeared since 1969 in *The New York Times* and since 1972 in some 70 other newspapers, magazines and journals. Although the data base increases at a weekly rate of more than 3300 summaries of articles, and subscribers and usage have increased dramatically, the operation took a number of years to become profitable, losing $1.6 million in 1976 and $900,000 in 1977. In 1978, this loss was reduced to $250,000 and the service was in

Table 6.1: Major U.S. Online Bibliographic or Full-Text Data Base Services

Search Service	Name of Retrieval System	Number of Data Bases, 1980
Bibliographic Retrieval Services (BRS)	STAIRS	38
New York Times Information Bank (NYTIB)		6
Lockheed Information Systems	DIALOG	120
National Library of Medicine	ELHILL	16
System Development Corp. (SDC) Search Service	ORBIT	80
Dow Jones	News/Recall Service	6
Mead	LEXIS	2*

*Mead Data Central speaks of its full-text NEXIS and LEXIS services as "electronic libraries" rather than data bases. LEXIS contains federal and state law libraries from several types of courts. NEXIS, at last count, contained a library of at least 50 publications, wire services and newspapers.
Source: Knowledge Industry Publications, Inc.

the black in 1979. The Times' experience amply demonstrates that launching a machine-readable data base is an expensive undertaking, and one that requires a major long-term commitment and sustained support. The New York Times Information Service has since introduced a number of new data bases in the news area, such as MEDAB on the Middle East, KIT which tracks key issues and, in response to the current groundswell for "friendly systems" that are easy to use, has made available an enhanced full-text version of *The New York Times*. New York Times Information Service plans to add other types of data bases soon. New York Times Information Service revenues were estimated to be between $8 and $9 million in 1980.

BRS, SDC and Lockheed offer many data bases in scientific and technical fields, some of which overlap. Their offerings are directed at academic and also special libraries. Details on these appear in the profiles in Chapter 9. It should be noted here, however, that all three are distributors rather than producers of data bases, while The New York Times Information Bank is both a producer and a distributor. Chemical Abstracts Service entered the online data base business at the end of 1980 making one huge data base of chemical substance information available on CAS's own system.

Another data base is the Dow Jones News Retrieval Service. The computerized news system enables users, primarily stock brokerage firms and banks, to call up on a video screen or teleprinter current news items as well as those published during the previous 90 days by Dow Jones newspapers, principally the *Wall Street Journal*. Dow Jones introduced in mid-1977 the lower cost Dow Jones News/Retrieval Service. It utilizes time-share computer terminals and provides up-to-the-minute stock quotations. The time-share service is designed primarily for corporations and brokerage houses. Recently, Dow Jones has begun to aim at a broader market by making its data bases accessible via lower cost personal computers such as the Apple.

Mead Data Central, a subsidiary of Mead Corp., offers a legal data base called LEXIS, whose prime market is lawyers and accountants. West Publishing Co., a major publisher of legal books, offers a competing service called WESTLAW. Mead's LEXIS system has added the NYTIB data base as well as ABI/INFORM, a move seen as an attempt to expand its customer and revenue base. In 1980 Mead Data Central started a new online service called NEXIS which covers newspapers and periodicals of general interest in full-text format.

Also in 1980, Source Telecomputing Corporation (STC) which offers a low-cost online service containing data bases of consumer information, electronic games, electronic mail and computer programs, reached an agreement with OCLC whereby the Source service is being offered to

THE SHRINKING LIBRARY DOLLAR

libraries. STC is a subsidiary of the Reader's Digest Association. And the timesharing computer services company, CompuServe, purchased by H&R Block in 1980, also offers an online consumer information service that includes electronic home delivery of the news content of 13 major U.S. newspapers.

In general, those search services which provide many data bases, e.g., Lockheed, SDC, BRS, have a better chance to increase revenues and improve profitablity than those which carry one or only a few data bases, because they can spread their costs as well as generate higher revenues.

The Library Market for Online Bibliographic Services and Other Data Bases

As previously noted, the number of publicly available bibliographic data bases had grown to some 528 in 1979, over 259 of them produced in the United States. Another indication of growth in this market is the 116 million bibliographic references in the U.S., Canada and Europe available for online searching in 1979, up 132% from the 50 million in 1977.[3] The number of online searches rose from an estimated 700,000 in 1974 to 2.5 million in 1978 and to an estimated 4 million in 1979; a 60% increase. Growth in the number of data bases offered by the major providers of search services has also been rapid. Lockheed, for example, had 18 data bases in 1974, and more than 115 at the end of 1980.[4]

Based on the estimated 4 million searches sold in 1979 at an average cost of $28 per search, the market for such searches was $112 million. Projecting only a 50% increase in the number of searches from 1979 to 1981 would indicate an estimated 6 million searches. Based on an average cost of $28 per search, the 1981 market for such services is $168 million. Much of this expenditure, however, is passed on to the end user. Company research budgets and government grants pay the bill in most cases. In 1981, the corporate market, which includes corporate libraries, is said to out number the library as a data base customer by three to one. Thus, if one-third of this total represents library expenditures, the library market for online bibliographic services is more than $56 million in 1981.

Despite the positive signs for growth in this market, and the benefits to be derived by libraries from offering data base services, the market has also brought problems. Two basic ones are the need for someone to serve as an information intermediary in the library for those who wish to utilize online systems and the high cost of individualized data base services. The latter inspired a price war in the field, which erupted when BRS entered the market in early 1977 and challenged SDC and Lockheed by offering substantially lower prices. The advent of online services has also raised philosophical questions for libraries, many of which view

The Library Market for Systems

charging for such services a threat to free libraries.

Developments in telecommunications technology have greatly aided the growth of data bases, and promise continued increases in usage in the years ahead. Because of "value-added networks" like Telenet and Tymnet, customers can obtain access to major data bases with only a local phone call, with the cost of communications representing a manageable, though not insignificant, portion of total costs. As advanced satellite communications systems like Satellite Business Systems (a joint venture of IBM, Comsat and Aetna Casualty and Life) go into operation, it will be possible to communicate with central data banks by means of roof-top terminals located in an office building or library. This will all but eliminate local and long distance telephone connections for certain kinds of data transmission.

EQUIPMENT AND SYSTEMS

The library of the 1970s and 1980s has turned increasingly to advanced technology equipment and systems in an effort to cut long-range costs, increase efficiency and cut book and other material losses. Two of the outgrowths of this quest have come in the form of automated circulation systems and book theft security systems, which represented a market of well over $36 million in 1981. While this market is still small in comparison with, for example, the book and periodical markets, it is a growing market and offers a glimpse of the library of the future.

Automated Cirulation Systems

Automating circulation functions is attractive to libraries for a variety of reasons. First, it can eliminate clerical chores and free library staff for other services. Second, it can effect speedy and efficient circulation transactions while simultaneously providing up-to-date records of loans, due dates and borrowers. Third, and perhaps most important to libraries, it offers the prospect of long-range cost control over operation of the library circulation system.

On the negative side, the cost to libraries can be substantial, whether they choose a circulation package or develop a "home grown" system. Almost no system can be installed for less than $100,000, and while the capital expense can be spread over a period of five to 10 years, there are ongoing associated costs throughout the life of the system. These can include the cost of telecommunications, where necessary, to link remote terminals to the minicomputer or the minicomputer to the host computer or both. In addition, maintenance and service must be included in the cost estimate, as well as supplies, installation costs and controls required

THE SHRINKING LIBRARY DOLLAR

to keep the system operating, e.g., temperature and humidity controls.

In addition to cost, some libraries which have opted for automated circulation systems have encountered various other problems, including maintenance difficulties and slow response time; a particular headache for systems that serve geographically separated libraries which make heavy interloan demands on one another.

Libraries have tapped a variety of financial sources to pay for these systems, including revenue sharing and LSCA funds. In general, libraries interested in automating must make the decision to opt for long-term rather than short-term benefits, measuring expected savings against the size of the investment needed and the alternative ways in which the money being considered for automated circulation could be invested.

Packaged Systems for Automating Circulation

Competition has become intense among purveyors of packaged systems, with CL Systems, Inc. (Newton, MA), the major supplier, being sued by another system marketer, DataPhase (Kansas City, MO). DataPhase's $5.7 million suit, filed June 1, 1978, charged CL Systems with making "malicious and fraudulent" statements about DataPhase. It also alleged violations of the antitrust laws by CL Systems. CLS denied all these allegations and called DataPhase's action a "sour grapes lawsuit." As the litigation dragged on and expenses mounted without a settlement drawing nearer, the two vendors finally agreed out-of-court in March 1981, to drop all legal proceedings.

At the end of April 1981, CL Systems claimed 292 of its LIBS 100 automated circulation systems were in operation in libraries in the U.S., Canada and Australia. In addition, it reported signing up 9 library systems which will have circulation systems installed later in 1981.

DataPhase, meanwhile, listed 26 public libraries, 12 academic libraries and several government libraries (including the National Agricultural Library in Beltsville, MD), as customers at the end of the first quarter of 1981.

While these two vendors of automated systems dominated developments, a number of other companies made inroads in the automated circulation systems market. Gaylord Brothers, Inc. (Syracuse, NY) won two large installations; a 42-terminal set-up at the Public Library of Columbus and Franklin County (Ohio) and an 83-terminal system at the Queens Borough Public Library (Jamaica, NY). Another notable event was the decision by 3M Co. to abandon its automated circulation system after a well-publicized failure at Princeton to get the system working properly. Decicom also left the field in 1979. That same year a newcomer, Geac Ltd. of Canada, made its presence

The Library Market for Systems

known with its Geac 8000 minicomputer system being selected for use by Connecticut's Capitol Region Library Council and Southwestern Library System as well as by the University of Arizona. Geac listed 10 U.S. installations by May 1981.

Manufacturers of automated circulation systems are listed in Table 6.2. Companies are listed alphabetically rather than ranked by number of installations.

Custom Designed Systems

Home grown circulation systems, such as those in use at many research libraries, rely on a central computer, which processes daily records of circulation systems. Home grown systems depend upon access to a computer. For a research or academic library, the host computer could be at the university computer center; for a public library, it could be a government or commercial computer.

An advantage of this type of system is that libraries can design systems which are individually tailored to their needs, or systems that do exactly what they want them to do. Libraries opting for custom developed automated circulation systems must also design software that will be compatible with the existing computer, build their own data bases and select compatible hardware for their circulation terminals. Many custom systems rely on IBM equipment and are dependent on IBM 360 or 370 host computers for batch processing of circulation files.

Examples of custom systems include the one in use at the Regenstein Library at the University of Chicago, which employs a circulation terminal operated with a light pen that reads coded labels on books and patron identification cards. The library has software specially designed for its own needs as part of a total data base system that encompasses cataloging, acquisitions and circulation. Another in-house circulations system was implemented by the Macon/Bibb County Public Library in Georgia using IBM and NCR hardware; it was assembled at a cost of $18,000.

IBM has recently begun to market its DOBIS/LEUVEN automated circulation and cataloging system which was developed in Europe and marketed only in Canada. Maintaining its usual low profile, IBM does not release the names of libraries installing the system. However, one recent installation took place at the Austin (TX) Public Library.

Market for Automated Circulation Systems

Estimates of the size of the automated circulation systems market

THE SHRINKING LIBRARY DOLLAR

Table 6.2: Manufacturers of Automated Circulation Systems and Number of Installations in Operation, 1981

Name of System, Manufacturer, Address	Total No. of Installations
Checkpoint/Plessey Checkpoint Systems, Inc. 110 East Gloucester Pike Barrington, NJ 08007	4 U.S., 2 Canada
CLASSIC Cincinnati Electronics 2630 Glendale-Milford Rd. Cincinnati, OH 45241	6 U.S.
LIBS 100 CL Systems Inc. 81 Norwood Ave. Newton, MA 02160	292
DataPhase Systems, Inc. 4528 Belleview Kansas City, MO 64111	41
Gaylord Automated Circulation Control System Gaylord Library Systems, a division of Gaylord Bros. PO Box 61 Syracuse, NY 13201	10, plus 1 demonstration site
Geac Canada, Ltd. 350 Steelcase Rd. West Markham, Ontario L3R1B3, Canada	10 U.S., 7 Canada
Innovated Systems 10920 Indian Trail Suite 301 Dallas, TX 75229	1
SCICON Systems Control, Inc. 1801 Page Mill Rd. Palo Alto, CA 94304	2
ULISYS Universal Library Systems Ltd. Suite 202, 60 St. Clair Ave. East Toronto, Ontario M4T 1N5, Canada	6 U.S., 3 Canada

Source: Knowledge Industry Publications, Inc.

The Library Market for Systems

vary, but at the end of 1980, it was an active, highly competitive marketplace.

Richard Boss, in a study in 1978 on automated circulation for the American Library Association, estimated that from late 1973 until the end of 1976, the online systems market totaled about $10 million.[5] Boss estimated that in 1977 another $10 million worth of systems were sold while for 1978 the total came to $19 million. Boss also projected 1979 sales to reach $36 million. Boss says his estimates were based on input from vendors of automated circulation systems.

CL Systems alone had revenues of $11.7 million for the fiscal year ending June 30, 1980, up from $8.4 million a year earlier. CL Systems was expecting revenues of $12.5 million for fiscal 1981 or a growth rate of close to 7%, and projects revenues of $14.0 million for fiscal 1982, or a growth rate of 12%.

Assuming perhaps 60 installations a year (CL Systems had more than 50 installations itself in 1978) and an average system cost of $300,000, the market for automated circulation systems in 1980 was around $18 million. (Boss also bases his estimates on a $300,000 average cost.) Based on current growth estimates by companies involved in the market, Knowledge Industry Publications believes a realistic projection is for $20 million in 1981.[6]

Theft Prevention/Electronic Security Systems

If the 1970s and early 1980s was the era of automated circulation systems, it was also the era of electronic security systems in libraries. And, in at least two instances (Knogo Corp. and Gaylord Bros.), purveyors of security systems were involved in automated circulation systems as well, thus acknowledging the desirability of combining the two kinds of equipment. Knogo Corp. unveiled the first combination book security and automated circulation system in the library market at the 1978 American Library Association midwinter meeting. Knogo, which had been exclusively in the security business, already had 150 book detection systems. Gaylord is active on both the electronic security system and automated circulation system fronts with existing systems in both areas.

However, Checkpoint, (which had entered the circulation system market) no longer markets the Plessey circulation system and thus is active only in the security area.

In other changes in the library security market, the Library Bureau of Herkimer, NY, was acquired by General Nucleonics Inc., of which Sentronic is a division.

The move by libraries toward acquiring book theft prevention systems

THE SHRINKING LIBRARY DOLLAR

arose because of the increase in book theft in libraries and its huge cost to these institiutions. Loss rates of between 2% and 15% have been described as not uncommon, and even a loss of 1% annually in U.S. libraries, which house an estimated 1.5 billion volumes, is staggering. Projecting a loss of 1% of 1.5 billion volumes amounts to some 15 million books. Assuming an average replacement cost of $15 per book, the total annual replacement figure comes to $225 million, or more than 10% of what libraries spend annually.[7]

In view of these losses, libraries are moving toward theft prevention measures, which can be as simple as guards and as complicated as sophisticated electronic security systems. Systems currently in use in U.S. libraries operate on differing principles. Checkpoint, for example, is based on radio frequency, Knogo and Gaylord/Magnavox on electromagnetism, Sentronic on magnetism. Bypass systems, which employ permanently sensitized tags, are most often used in public libraries, while full-circulating systems are employed in institutions where users frequently return with previously charged-out materials. The latter are more costly since special units are needed to deactivate and reactivate the detector tags which are placed on library materials.

Electronic security systems are far less costly than automated circulation systems, with the average cost at around $14,000 per system. As with circulation systems, various rental plans are also available. In general, the 3M/1850 and Book-Mark systems are the most expensive, while Checkpoint is the least costly. Table 6.3 lists companies operating in the electronic security system market in 1980. The largest is 3M, followed by Checkpoint and Knogo.

Based on approximately 500 installations, the 1981 market for electronic security systems is roughly $7 to $8 million. All types of libraries are customers for these systems. Among a partial lisiting of 3M's installations, for example, are 34 special libraries, 27 public libraries, 94 universities, 35 colleges and 45 high schools.[8]

Although technology involved in such systems is still imperfect (in some cases library patrons can locate and remove detector tags, as well as foil some systems by carrying magnets), it has been estimated that the systems can reduce losses by 75% to 90%. In view of the relatively low cost and high return gained by libraries which employ the systems, they should experience steady growth in the 1980s.

CATALOGING AND PROCESSING SERVICES

A number of companies as well as the Library of Congress provide cataloging and processing services, which give individual libraries an

The Library Market for Systems

Table 6.3: Leading Electronic Security System Marketers and Number of Installations in Operation, 1978

Company & Address	Total Number of Installations
Checkpoint Systems, Inc. PO Box 188 550 Grove Rd. Thorofare, NJ 08086	more than 1500
Gaylord Library Systems PO Box 4901 Syracuse, NY 13221	more than 90
Knogo Corp. 100 Tec Street Hicksville, NY 11801	200 - 250
Sentronic International (Div. of General Nucleonics, Inc.) PO Box 116 Brunswick, OH 44212	at least 100
3M Co. Library Systems, 220-9E 3M Center St. Paul, MN 55144	more than 3000

Source: Alice H. Bahr, *Book Theft and Security Systems, 1981-82* (White Plains, NY: Knowledge Industry Publications, Inc., 1981).

alternative to performing these tasks themselves. These services can be offered either manually or by means of an online computer. In a number of cases, both types of service are offered by the same firm. Cataloging and processing services are a growing part of the library technology market, despite some resistance by librarians who feel that they must catalog and process themselves according to their own specifications.

The Library of Congress

A big boost to the provision of cataloging and processing services came from the Library of Congress' development of the MARC Distribution Service, instituted in 1969. MARC (Machine-Readable Cataloging) provides machine-readable records for many types of publications in a variety of languages. Subscribers, who numbered about 67 at the end of 1980, include major academic libraries, networks like OCLC and RLIN and commercial firms. They receive weekly or monthly computer tapes, at prices ranging from $1000 to $10,000 per year, depending on the type of record required. Vendors providing cataloging and processing services say that the institution of MARC not only lowers the cost of providing services to their customers but gives them an acceptable format to offer libraries.

In addition to developing MARC, the Library of Congress is a major supplier of catalog cards, selling about 2.4 million card sets annually at 45 cents each, for revenues of $1.1 million. In what the library refers to as the "old days," it printed catalog cards via a combination of phototypesetting and offset printing and sent them by mail to libraries. By the end of 1978, however, it was printing cards on-demand by means of its Card Automated Reproduction Demand System (CARDS) developed by Xerox Electro-Optical Systems (Pasadena, CA) in response to its need to respond more quickly to card orders and also for more cost-effective operations. The CARDS system uses laser, xerographic and computer technology to produce MARC cards, and is linked to existing computer software and systems developed and used by the Library of Congress' Cataloging Distribution Service since 1970.

There was considerable speculation about the longevity of CARDS once *Anglo-American Cataloging Rules, Second Edition (AACR 2),* are implemented and the Library of Congress card catalog is closed. Having been delayed once in September 1978, LC closed its card catalog on Jan. 2, 1981. Some librarians look to the closing of the catalog to mean the exact opposite: i.e., the opening of the catalog, as libraries become more sensitive to individual needs and break away from Library of Congress standards. For its part, LC insists it is not closing the catalog but simply starting a new one, actually two new catalogs. One will house all entries which are in machine-readable form, the other will be for non-computer entries. The Library of Congress maintains that it will continue to produce cards and maintain card operations as long as there are libraries that want them, and as long as Congress appropriates funds for this service.

A new and relatively inexpensive hardware/software system by Informatics provides Library of Congress catalogs records in machine-readable form. When added to Informatics' MINI MARC system, a printer generates complete headed card sets.

Not-for-Profit Networks

Not-for-profit networks, including OCLC, RLIN, University of Toronto Library Automation System (UTLAS) and Washington Library Network (WLN), are also vendors of cataloging and processing services for libraries, providing them on a computerized, online basis.

The growth of OCLC from an Ohio network to a nationwide computer utility is synonymous with the spurt of computerized activity in cataloging and processing services which characterized the last half of the 1970s. OCLC's revenues, all of which can be classified as catalog-related, reached almost $28 million for the year ended June 30, 1980. OCLC reported production of 113.2 million cards in fiscal 1980, three times the 39.6 million produced in 1976. Its membership, catalog card production revenue and related services also increased dramatically in the second half of the 1970s and early 1980s. There are more than 7 million records in the OCLC data base, and more than 2260 libraries using its services. There were almost 4000 terminals hooked into the online system in April 1981.

Individual libraries spend considerable sums of money on OCLC services annually. A medium-sized library that catalogs 20,000 items a year can easily spend upwards of $28,000 a year on OCLC services.

BALLOTS, another online technical processing system, became an independent unit of Stanford University in 1977. By mid-1978, more than 50 libraries were using BALLOTS as a shared cataloging system and over 100 others were using it to search for bibliographic data. When Stanford joined the Research Libraries Group in the fall of 1978, BALLOTS became the Research Libraries Information network or RLIN. RLIN presently has 23 owner/members, plus a number of special members. Many other libraries of all types use the "search only" services of RLIN.

In addition to OCLC and RLG, UTLAS, used by more than 200 libraries in Canada, and WLN offer online cataloging and processing services. UTLAS is not as widely known in the United States as OCLC or RLG, while WLN is the newest and is still the smallest online network. In 1979, RLG and WLN announced plans to cooperate and share data bases.

Commercial Firms

In addition to the Library of Congress and not-for-profit networks, there are a number of commercial firms which offer cataloging and processing services. These include wholesalers, publishers and specialized firms, some of which go to great lengths to provide libraries what they want in these areas.

Baker & Taylor, for example, the largest book wholesaler to libraries, claims that more than 5000 libraries utilize its cataloging and processing services, which it promotes on the basis of cost saving and convenience. Complete processing costs $.99 per item from Baker & Taylor, which the company claims is less than 15% of what an individual library would incur. Baker & Taylor offers a variety of options in cataloging, including the abridged Dewey classification, the Dewey classification with Library of Congress format and subject headings, and a Library of Congress

THE SHRINKING LIBRARY DOLLAR

classification with format and subject headings. The company claims broad title coverage, with cataloging data bases including more than 1 million records, comprised of the MARC data base of over 1 million entries and its own data base of over 300,000 Dewey/LC and Dewey/Sears records.

In addition to the complete processing service for $.99, Baker & Taylor offers other options at lower cost (jacket and kit, unattached; attached kit, etc.). It also offers theft detection devices at $.40 per book.

In addition to annual cataloging and processing, Baker & Taylor offers a number of automated services for libraries under the trade name LIBRIS. These include BATAB, an automated buying system; machine-readable catalog records, and conversion of card catalogs to computer output microfilm (COM).

Another wholesaler, Brodart, provides custom services for catalog conversion and book and computer output microfilm production, utilizing the MARC data base as well as several other large bibliographic data bases. Brodart charges the same for complete processing as Baker & Taylor, $.99. Brodart also has an online system for some acquisition tasks, IROS (Instant Response Ordering System). (See Brodart profile in Chapter 9 for details on IROS.)

Still another wholesaler, Blackwell North America (BNA), has taken over the automated bibliographic system developed by the Richard Abel Co., acquired by Blackwell in 1975. BNA's data base consists of the MARC data, MARC records from other countries, records input by its own staff and the University of California Union Catalog Supplement.

Book publishers can also offer cataloging and processing services, which could provide an enticement to direct sales that otherwise might go to wholesalers. Grosset & Dunlap, for example, a major juvenile book publisher, offers fully processed library editions for an additional $.95.

A number of specialized companies also provide libraries with cataloging and processing services. Among them are Inforonics, which has an online catalog support system using MARC data. In addition, three companies offer microform catalog data to libraries seeking to speed up cataloging processes without automating: Information Design, Inc. (Menlo Park, CA), which offers Cardset; Marc Applied Research Co. (Washington, DC), which sells Marcfiche; and 3M Library Services' MCRS, formerly offered by Information Dynamics.

Market for Cataloging and Processing Services

The 1981 market for cataloging and processing services is estimated at $51 million. This estimate is based on some $6 million annually in manual card production, such as that performed by wholesalers, specialized companies and the Library of Congress, and another $45 million in computerized cataloging and processing services. Along with online reference searching, the market for computerized cataloging and processing services was by far the largest single market for computer-based technology in libraries at the end of 1980. If OCLC, the largest supplier, is a guide to market growth, revenues from this activity are growing at 47% annually.

SUMMARY

The library market for automated services and equipment was estimated at $134.5 million in 1981. Unlike materials budgets, this segment of the library market is vital and growing.

The growth of library networks was a phenomenon of the 1960s and 1970s. Many library functions, including cataloging, acquisitions and interlibrary loans, are adaptable to shared network processing.

Online bibliographic data base services as well as other data bases are provided by academic and special libraries and, in some cases, public libraries. The number of machine-readable data bases more than tripled between 1975 and 1978, from slightly over 100 to more than 360. The number of data bases increased 46.7% to 528 between 1978 and 1979.

Data base producers include the New York Times Information Bank, Chemical Abstracts Service, Engineering Index and Congressional Information Service, among others. Online vendors, or distributors, include Bibliographic Retrieval Services, Lockheed Information Systems, National Library of Medicine and System Development Corp. which have multiple data bases. The New York Times Information Bank and Dow Jones each had six data bases when this report was completed.

The library market for online bibliographic services was estimated at over $56 million in 1981.

The market for automated circulation systems and book theft security systems was estimated to be well over $27 million in 1981, with circulation systems accounting for some $20 million and book theft and security systems another $7 to $8 million.

Automated circulation systems are of two types; home grown or custom designed systems, and packaged. In the market for packaged systems, which is highly competitive, CL Systems is the leader; it claimed 292 installations at the end of April 1981.

Libraries have moved to book theft prevention systems because of the increase in book theft in libraries and its huge cost to these institutions. 3M Company was the leading marketer of such systems in 1981.

In addition to the Library of Congress, a number of companies provide cataloging and processing services, which can be offered either manually or by means of an online computer.

Not-for-profit networks, including OCLC, RLIN and others, are vendors of cataloging and processing services for libraries, which they provide on an online basis. Commercial firms including wholesalers and specialized companies also provide these services.

The 1981 market for cataloging and processing services was estimated at $51 million, including $6 million in manual card production and another $45 million in computerized cataloging and processing services.

FOOTNOTES

1. For a complete description of the current developments in library networks, see Susan K. Martin, *Library Networks, 1981-82* (White Plains, NY: Knowledge Industry Publications, Inc., 1981).
2. Ryan E. Hoover, ed., *The Library and Information Manager's Guide to Online Services* (White Plains, NY: Knowledge Industry Publications, Inc., 1980).
3. Martha E. Williams, *Bulletin of the American Society for Information Science,* 1980.
4. Ibid.
5. Richard W. Boss, "Circulation Systems: The Options," *Library Technology Reports,* 1978.
6. For a complete discussion of these systems, see Alice Harrison Bahr, *Automated Library Circulation Systems, 1979-1980* (White Plains, NY: Knowledge Industry Publications, Inc., 1979).
7. Alice Harrison Bahr, *Book Theft and Library Security Systems, 1981-82* (White Plains, NY: Knowledge Industry Publications, Inc., 1981).
8. Ibid.

7
The Library Market for Audiovisual and Other Materials

In addition to print materials—books and periodicals—libraries are a market for audiovisual materials, equipment and furniture, bindings and microforms. These nonprint markets have grown at different rates in the 1970s, and face less than buoyant futures in the 1980s.

AUDIOVISUAL MATERIALS

Audiovisual materials sales rose 51.4% from $167.0 million in 1970 to $252.9 million in 1977. The total for 1977 was below the $273.0 million in sales for 1974 and the $276.9 million recorded in 1975. Despite mid-1970s predictions of dramatic growth, sales of audiovisual materials lagged because of declines in federal funding and constricted budgets in major sales markets such as elementary and high schools and public libraries. In 1979 alone, sales in half of the 10 categories in Table 7.1 declined from 1978 levels, as total sales posted a tiny 2.1% gain. From 1975 to 1979, total sales for audiovisual materials decreased 6.9%, with all but two categories showing declines. Recorded video tapes, still relatively new, are also one of the few bright spots in the business, and multimedia kits posted a slight gain of 2.9% from 1975-1979.

The BISG forecasts that audiovisual materials will become a smaller percentage of library purchases between 1976 and 1984. It predicts a small 5.9% increase in total sales in the four-year period from 1980 to 1984 despite the 6.9% decline recorded by the Association of Media Producers from 1975 to 1979. (See Table 7.1.)

Sales did not fare well in the library market in the 1970s, and their performance into the early 1980s is not expected to improve substantially. School libraries, the major library market for audiovisual materials, will acquire 14.5% fewer audiovisual materials in 1984 than they did in 1976, according to Book Industry Study Group projections, which foresee a decline in dollars from $78.4 million to $67.0 million in this period. Audiovisual materials acquisitions are also expected to decrease in

THE SHRINKING LIBRARY DOLLAR

Table 7.1: Audiovisual Materials Sales by Product Format, 1975-1979

Format	1975	1976	1977	1978	1979	% change 1975-1979
16mm films	$ 64.3	$ 62.3	$ 69.0	$ 74.0	$ 77.5	+ 8.7%
Prerecorded video tapes & rental income	7.0	6.0	6.0			
8mm films (silent)	5.3	3.6	3.0	2.5	2.7	− 57.1
8mm films (sound)	1.0	0.4				
Silent filmstrips	12.0	9.0	9.5	6.0	71.0	− 12.9
Sound filmstrips	69.5	62.5	61.5	64.0		
Prepared overhead transparencies	5.0	4.0	3.5	3.0	2.9	− 42.0
2 × 2 slides	3.0	2.8	2.6	2.5	2.1	− 3.0
Records	5.4	5.0	4.8	5.0	5.0	− 7.4
Prerecorded tapes (reel-to-reel)	2.0	1.2				
Prerecorded tapes (cassettes)	17.1	16.0	15.5	15.0	14.5	− 24.1
Study prints	11.0	9.5	9.0	8.5	7.5	− 31.8
Multimedia kits	52.5	45.6	48.5	52.5	54.0	+ 2.9
Games, manipulatives and realia	21.8	19.0	20.0	19.5	20.5	− 6.0
Total	$276.9	$246.9	$252.9	$252.5	$257.7	− 6.9

Source: Association of Media Producers, 1980.

The Library Market for Audiovisual and Other Materials

academic libraries between 1976 and 1984, from $15.3 million to $13.1 million, a drop of 14.4%. They will also decline from 26.7% to 14.2% of all school library acquisitions.

By contrast, public libraries' acquisitions of audiovisual materials are forecast to rise dramatically from $14.3 million in 1976 to $27.7 million in 1984, up 93.7% Finally, special libraries are expected to increase acquisitions of audiovisual materials substantially between 1976 and 1984, from $10.3 million in 1976 to $16.1 million in 1984, a 56.3% rise. Where school and academic libraries accounted for 79% of library purchases of audiovisual materials in 1976, BISG predicts their share will fall to 65% in 1984. Public and special libraries are predicted to make 35% of library audiovisual purchases in 1984 vs. 21% in 1976.

Unfortunately for companies selling audiovisual materials to libraries, special and public libraries (the two library markets where sales will rise) represent smaller customers for audiovisual materials. In 1980, for example, only 30% of audiovisual materials acquisitions were made by special and public libraries.

As a percentage of total materials acquisitions, audiovisual expenditures are small and declining. Where audiovisual materials acquisitions represented 10.4% of total materials acquisitions in 1976, this percentage was forecast to drop to 5.6% by 1984.

Channels of Distribution for Audiovisual Materials

Audiovisual materials are sold in a variety of ways: by direct sales force, by direct mail and, in some cases, by telephone. They are generally not sold by wholesalers. Experiments involving these middlemen selling audiovisual materials to libraries in the mid-1970s proved uniformly dismal, mainly because the largest publishers of media materials, such as Encyclopaedia Britannica Educational Corp. and Society for Visual Education (SVE) (Singer), preferred to sell direct. Baker & Taylor, which pushed its "Quick Lists" of audiovisual materials in the mid-1970s and lined up an impressive list of companies for which it distributed, considers its inability to attract the major suppliers of the industry and its lack of success in wholesaling audiovisual materials a major disappointment.

The largest audiovisual materials companies, like Encyclopaedia Britannica, SVE, Time-Life Films and Films Inc., maintain direct sales forces, an avenue of sales which is becoming too expensive for many smaller companies. SVE, for example, had 80 salespeople calling on schools and libraries in 1979, selling the company's filmstrips and multimedia materials for the elementary level. Encyclopaedia Britannica

THE SHRINKING LIBRARY DOLLAR

had some 50 salespeople who sold reference materials as well as audiovisual materials to school and public libraries. Films Inc., which claims to be the largest company in the field of nontheatrical film rentals and in the sale of film and tape products to the educational market, has a library catalog listing over 1500 documentaries and short subjects selected specially for public libraries and educational institutions. Sales are made by three direct reps and three telephone reps.

Sales expenses are a major item for media publishers, accounting for 17.3% of net sales by audiovisual companies in 1979, the second largest expense after cost of materials sold.

Audiovisual materials companies are very dependent on reviews, and will basically try to get reviews anywhere they can. Publications which review media programs include *Booklist* and a number of American Library Association journals and educational journals such as *Learning* and *Media & Methods.*

Audiovisual materials are generally made available to libraries on a 30-day "on approval" basis. This is true of both 16mm films and sound filmstrip and multimedia formats.

Leading Audiovisual Publishers

Almost without exception, the leading audiovisual publishers tend to be parts of much larger companies. Their sales patterns have been discouraging in the late 1970s, because of softness in the overall audiovisual materials industry; and since a number of companies have been sold or reoriented away from education and library markets. For example, Guidance Associates is an audiovisual company which was sold by Harcourt Brace Jovanovich to The Center for the Humanities in September 1978 for $2 million. Guidance, a respected name in the media materials industry, was not profitable in 1978, according to HBJ. McGraw-Hill tried different forms of surgery on it ailing films division in the late 1970s, first trimming its films sales force in late 1976, later consolidating its film operations with CRM Films in DelMar, CA and announcing that it would concentrate on business and training markets. Further reorganization took place in 1981, and resulted in Tratec and Edutronics (in the school division) reporting to the International Book Co. and CRM Films in the McGraw-Hill Book Co.

Leading publishers of audiovisual materials for the library market include Encyclopaedia Britannica Educational Corp., Time-Life Films and Learning Corp. of America.

The Library Market for Audiovisual and Other Materials

Assessment of Library Needs for Audiovisual Materials

Libraries do not acquire enough audiovisual materials, according to *The National Inventory of Library Needs—1975,* which identified gaps in nonprint materials collections in public libraries, school library/media centers and academic libraries.

For public libraries, the *National Inventory* said nonprint holdings in total were well above the indicated needs, "but holdings of nonprint are so concentrated that other public libraries have gaps in nonprint holdings which total more than 10 million titles." In a suggestion which would warm the hearts of all audiovisual publishers who struggled through the 1970s, the *National Inventory* calculated that it would take an expenditure of $100 million, at 1974 price levels, to bring these collections up to minimum levels. The report estimated that nonprint collections in public libraries were more than 45 million items, of which audiovisual materials accounted for 8.3 million.

According to the *National Inventory,* there are "striking differences among the levels and types of standards currently applied to public service in the states," which, in turn, affect acquisitions and collections. It said variations in standards are largest in the area of audiovisual materials. While most states set no standards, several do, including Maryland, which recommends up to 800 films plus access to 1500 more through the regional resource center, and Florida, which stipulates 500 film titles or one per 1000 population, whichever is greater.

In public school library/media centers, which, as pointed out in Chapter 2 experienced dramatic growth between 1964 and 1974, about 100 million nonprint items were held in 1974. About 70% of these, or 70 million, were audiovisual materials, a number well below the estimated 1 billion items of nonprint materials that the *National Inventory* felt to be ideal.

Video in Libraries

Although video holds considerable promise for libraries, this promise was largely unfulfilled at the end of 1980. In *Video in Libraries: A Status Report, 1979-1980,* the use of video in libraries was seen as clearly in a state of flux. The main reason cited for lack of involvement in video was difficulty in determining exactly which services to provide and how to manage them, as well as problems of ongoing financial support.[1] Public access, a focal point of library video service in the early 1970s, has

THE SHRINKING LIBRARY DOLLAR

become less important than cable casting and staff training. In-house production was found to dominate the use of library-owned video equipment. Program availability was still seen as a central problem.

Outlook for Audiovisual Materials Sales to Libraries

Numerous factors mitigate against an upturn in library acquisitions of audiovisual materials in the early 1980s. First, where federal funding in the 1960s and early 1970s helped create thousands of school libraries, the main source of library audiovisual purchases, the source of library funding took a turn for the worse with passage of the Education Amendments of 1974. Under this federal legislation, several programs important for audiovisual materials purchases, including Title II of the Elementary and Secondary Education Act and Title III of the National Defense Education Act, were consolidated into Title IV-B. The reduced funding in the new law resulted in audiovisual materials purchases reversing their previously upward spiral in 1976. The downward trend continued into 1980.

In effect, under the Education Amendment of 1974, Title IV-B funds were used for purposes which were formerly set forth under the separate titles. These include acquisition of school library resources, textbooks and other instructional materials; acquisition of instructional equipment and minor remodeling of space used for such equipment; and guidance, counseling and testing (GCT).

Since the 1974 Act gave local education agencies total discretion over how Title IV-B funds are dispersed among library/media purchases, equipment and GCT, libraries could end up receiving less money under the IV-B consolidation than under the separate Title II, in spite of increased funding within the consolidated program. While federal funding is a smaller percentage than the local and state share of library funding it is a major source of money for school libraries and for audiovisual materials.

In 1981, as indicated earlier, the Reagan administration proposed further cuts in funding as well as the use of block grants. In fall 1981, the block grant proposals were signed into law; thus a portion of the federal funds for school resources and performances will be lumped together and states will develop their own spending priorities. Dollars will no longer be earmarked for books and materials.

Second, audiovisual materials companies, once considered prime candidates for growth, have become a disappointment to their corporate parents. Thus, Harcourt Brace Jovanovich sold its Guidance Associates subsidiary, while Doubleday closed down Doubleday Multimedia, to name just two. In 1978 other major changes that took place among companies which compete in the audiovisual materials market included the retrenchment at Damon's educational division, the sale of Changing Times Education Service (Kiplinger) to EMC Corp. and the sale of Newsweek's multimedia product line to Educational Audiovisual Inc. More recently, Center for the Humanities acquired first Parent's Magazine Films and, in 1981, exclusive distribution rights to the films and filmstrips of Xerox Education Publications.

Third, forecasts for sales in the two library markets (school and academic) which accounted for more than 70% of library acquisitions of audiovisual materials in 1980 are discouraging. Sales in both of these markets are expected to show a decline between 1976 and 1984.

AUDIOVISUAL EQUIPMENT

Audiovisual equipment, such as 16mm film projectors and sound and silent filmstrips, is sold to libraries through dealers rather than manufacturers. Because a middleman is involved, it is more difficult to pinpoint sales trends in this area. However, given factors previously cited, such as a decline in library construction, consolidated rather than categorical programs for library materials and equipment purchases, and generally poor library funding conditions, it is fair to assume that sales of audiovisual equipment have probably experienced scant growth in libraries since the mid-1970s.

Some input on one major equipment category, 16mm projectors, can be gleaned from Hope Reports' figures. Hope, which includes libraries in the community agency market, says that total market was $2.8 million in 1976, $3.2 million in 1978 and down to $2.7 million in 1980. Libraries constitute about 40% to 50% of the community agency category, which also includes youth and other community organizations. Some 16% to 17% of public libraries have such projectors, Hope says.

In general, it is probably fair to say that libraries will look increasingly at nontraditional equipment, e.g., video and microform hardware, with much of library acquisitions of 16mm and sound filmstrip projectors being for replacement purposes. However, according to Hope Reports, expenditures for audio, video and all other media but film also dropped from $600,000 in 1979 to $500,000 in 1980. Thus, Hope believes that the drop in film expenditures was not as much a factor of libraries choosing new video offerings over films, but rather a reflection of budgetary factors.

THE SHRINKING LIBRARY DOLLAR

LIBRARY FURNITURE AND SUPPLIES

The library market for furniture and supplies was estimated to be between $50 and $60 million in 1980. This market can be divided into three separate categories. The first is a catalog market, in which library supply companies sell a variety of furniture and supplies ranging from wooden desks and shelves to catalog cabinets and cement. The second is a heavy furniture market, which often involves competitive bidding for heavy library furniture as well as the expenditure of capital dollars from library construction funds. The third is the steel shelving, as opposed to wood shelving, market.

The leading firm in the catalog market is Gaylord Brothers (Sycracuse, NY). Gaylord is also involved in the library systems market via its stake in the automated circulation system market.

Brodart (Williamsport, PA), a major library wholesaler, has a second line of business which involves library supplies and equipment. In fiscal 1980, 19% of Brodart's revenues came from this area, which has been suffering from slow growth in recent years. Although fiscal revenues in 1980 were ahead 30.2% over fiscal 1979, the increase is primarily attributable to the acquisition of Dimondstein and Josten's in late 1978 and early 1979. Brodart manufactures 55% of the supplies and equipment it sells in the library and retail markets, including a complete line of wood furniture manufactured in its Williamsport facility. It also sells book jacket covers, book repair materials, record cards and pockets, and electromechanical circulation control systems. It has more than 4000 items in its supplies and equipment catalog.

Demco, which was part of George Banta Co. until it was purchased by a group of company executives in the fourth quarter of 1978, is the third-ranked company in the library supply and equipment field.

In the heavy furniture market, which includes custom-designed furniture, the top company is Library Bureau (Herkimer, NY). Another company, Myrtle, has left the market and Josten's was experiencing difficulties in 1978, and as indicated above, was acquired by Brodart in March 1979. Other companies that sell heavy furniture include Buckstaff (Oshkosh, WI); Texwood Furniture Corp. (Austin, TX) and Brodart. In view of the depressed state of library construction through most of the 1970s, it is not surprising that companies competing in this market have experienced difficulties.

A third library furniture market exists for steel shelving and stacks, attractive to libraries because they are cheaper than the wood variety. Estey

Corp. (Red Bank, NJ) is considered the leader in this market, in which the Ames Division, Mohawk Valley Community Corp. (Vineland, NJ) and Andrew Wilson Co. (Lawrence, MA) are also involved.

The library market for furniture and supplies is likely to remain moribund as long as library budgets remain tight and construction projects are limited. Except for replacement supplies and equipment, the growth area in nonmaterials purchasing by libraries would seem to be in technology, including automated circulation and cataloging systems.

BINDINGS

The library market for bindings was estimated to be $55.1 million in 1980, and was expected to rise to $67.2 million by 1984. The largest segment of the market was the academic libraries, where binding acquisitions totaled about $27.1 million. Special libraries had binding acquisitions of $21.8 million. These two types of libraries thus accounted for almost 89% of all binding acquisitions by U.S. libraries in 1980.

Bindings can be mechanical or handbound. Many publishers have a special library edition of their books covered with a particularly durable binding. In addition to companies which are binding specialists, including book manufacturers, a large number of firms are suppliers of book binding materials, providing components such as adhesives, coated and laminated book covering materials as well as cloth. Large book binding suppliers include Alling and Cory/Canfield Papers (Long Island City, NY), Chicopee Industrial Textile Division (Milltown, NY), Holliston Mills (Hyannis, MA), and Permalin Products Corp. (Port Washington, NY).

MICROFORMS

Microfilm refers to films on which information has been photographed on a reduced scale. Microforms are defined as all information carriers (microfiche, jackets, aperture cards, ultrafiche, microprints) that use microfilm.[2] Estimates of the size of the library microform market in 1980 vary depending on the source.

For example, the Book Industry Study Group (BISG) estimated the market at $50.5 million in 1980, accounting for 3.1% of total library materials acquisitions. BISG predicted almost a 25% increase in microform acquisitions to $62.9 million in 1984.

But given the number of companies competing in the market, their revenues and the percentage of their sales which come from the library market, the amount of microform acquisitions could be as much as 30% to 40% higher. Xerox University Microfilms, indentified in Table 7.2 as the largest microform publisher, did an estimated $30 million in business in 1980, all from the library market. Information Handling Services, Bell & Howell's Micro Photo Division and Microfilming Corp. of America (New York Times) are also involved in this market, with revenues from several million dollars to $20 million or more. Totaling the revenues of these companies and allowing for some smaller companies' revenues would result in a total market of $56 million or more, according to Knowledge Industry Publications estimates. (See Table 7.2 for leading micropublishers.)

Academic and special libraries, the largest library users of microforms, accounted for an estimated 89% of total microform acquisitions in 1980, BISG figures show, with $45.0 million in expenditures. These institutions represent the heaviest purchasers of proliferating scientific and technical as well as other scholarly information. Academic libraries increased their total microform units by 73% to 106.6 units between 1973-1974 and 1976-1977 and housed 146.7 units in 1979-1980, a 40% increase. However, since 1978, special libraries have replaced academic libraries as the largest purchasers of microforms. Where academic libraries spent $15.9 million on microforms in 1976 vs. special library purchasers of $13.3 million, 1984 estimates peg adademic library microform expenditures at $25.9 million vs. special library purchases of $29.7 million.

In addition to the materials portion of the market, the library market for microforms includes the equipment or hardware which is compatible with microforms. This includes microfiche readers and boxes, shelves and cabinets to store microforms.

Uses of Microforms

Microforms offer a number of advantages to libraries, chief among which are cost and space savings. In the area of cost, for example, a ma-

Table 7.2: Leading Micropublishers in the Market

University Microfilms
Information Handling Services
Bell & Howell Micro Photo
N.Y. Times Microfilming Corp. of America
Princeton Microfilm Corp.
Readex Microprint Corp.

Source: Knowledge Industry Publications, Inc.

The Library Market for Audiovisual and Other Materials

jor publisher of journals, Pergamon Press, offers its journals on microfiche for 80% of the hard copy price, a distinct advantage to libraries in a time of rapidly rising periodical prices (see Chapter 5). In terms of space savings, it has been estimated that a microform catalog takes up only 2% of the room of the traditional hard copy catalog. In addition, microforms can offer protection against theft and deterioration, although, for security purposes, they are probably better adapted to closed stacks.

Traditional uses of microforms abound, and have been implemented from the lowest educational levels, i.e., elementary schools, to the most sophisticated research libraries. They include storing newspapers, such as *The New York Times* and *The Wall Street Journal,* magazines and journals on microforms rather than in their originally published state. Microforms are cheaper and easier to store than hard copies, binding expense is saved and handling is simplified.

Microforms are also utilized to store and preserve research materials, such as doctoral dissertations available in this format from Xerox University Microfilms and educational reports in microform from Educational Resources Information Center (ERIC).

Information of current interest to library patrons, including college catalogs and telephone books, is also increasingly being offered in microform. Examples here include the National Microform Library's microfiche collection of some 2000 college catalogs and Bell & Howell Micro Photo's Phonefiche, which represents 360 Bell System directories. Several companies also offer microform catalog data. (See Chapter 6.)

Microforms have also been adapted to a variety of innovative uses. The one which has gained the most attention in libraries, and is most often mentioned by suppliers of services to the library market, particularly wholesalers, is computer output microfilm (COM), which has applications for automated catalog production in libraries as well as other services. COM has been called the fastest growing segment of the micrographics industry.

Lockheed Missiles and Space Company's Technical Information Center was the first large-scale library user of COM catalogs, beginning in 1966. By mid-1978, there were at least 40 libraries, including Lockheed and the Yale University Library, that were producing COM catalogs. By 1980, the number exceeded 60 and was climbing steadily.

The closing of the Library of Congress card catalog and the implementation of *Anglo-American Cataloging Rules, Second Edition (AACR2)* (discussed in Chapter 6) in 1981 further enhanced the attractiveness of COM catalogs for libraries wishing to close their own catalogs. The University of California at Berkeley, for example, made a quick decision

THE SHRINKING LIBRARY DOLLAR

to close its card catalog for COM on January 5, 1981 because of the impact of absorbing *AACR 2* headings.

Micropublishers

There were over 55 micropublishers in 1981, as identified in *Literary Market Place*. In addition to these commercial firms, the U.S. government, through the Government Printing Office, and agencies such as ERIC, are involved in micropublishing.

The leading commercial micropublisher is Xerox University Microfilms (Ann Arbor, MI), part of Xerox Publishing, which had estimated revenues of $20 million in 1978, all from the library market. University Microfilms does publishing of out-of-print books and periodicals, monographs, dissertations and other documents by xerography, lithography, roll microfilm and microfiche.

Information Handling Services (IHS), an Indian Head Company located in Englewood, CO, had 1978 revenues of $40 million, a minority of them from the library market. IHS provides prepackaged and custom services on 8mm and 16mm roll microfilm and microfiche. Its micropublishing efforts include federal specifications and standards, product and vendor catalog data, and publications for industry, government and education as well as for libraries.

Bell & Howell, which is a micropublisher as well as a manufacturer of microform reading equipment, generated millions of dollars in revenues from its Micro Photo division in 1980. The division, located in Wooster, OH, micropublishes foreign and U.S. newspapers on 35mm film and periodicals and telephone directories on microfiche (Phonefiche). Additional micropublishing efforts include scholarly collections on 35mm microfilm and microfiche and newspaper indexes.

In addition to these publishers, other companies offer journals in microform, often at substantial savings to libraries. The American Chemical Society, for example, began placing specialized materials on microfilm in 1971, switching to microfiche in 1973 in reaction to demand for these materials. Pergamon Press (Elmsford, NY), which publishes professional and reference books as well as international business and scientific research journals, began offering simultaneous microfiche subscriptions to its 240 sci/tech, medical and educational journals in 1976, providing libraries with an option for significant cost savings: 80% of hard copy cost for fiche alone, 50% of hard copy cost for institutions ordering either fiche or film in addition to hard copy at full price.

The development of the micropublishing industry has spawned a number of publications which are directed at those interested in publications in the microform format. *Microform Review,* published bimonthly, reviews worldwide micropublications and provides information about micropublishing. The same company publishes *Guide to Microforms in Print, Microform Market Place* (distributed by R.R. Bowker) and *Micropublishers Trade List Annual.*

Publishers interested in micropublishing as well as librarians interested in acquiring micropublished projects are served by the coordinating function of the American Library Association's Resources and Technical Services Division Subcommittee on Micro-Publishing Projects.

Equipment for Microforms

Libraries that use microforms represent a market for the specialized equipment necessary to read material in this format. Major equipment costs include those of readers and reader printers. These cost around $500, depending on features, with fiche readers generally less expensive than their microfiche counterparts. Use of microforms may also require purchase of study carrels, at approximately $200 each, as well as shelves or cabinets where microforms are stored.

Manufacturers of microform viewing equipment tend to be those that also dominate the audiovisual equipment field. In addition to the Bell & Howell Micro Photo Division, industry leaders include Eastman Kodak and 3M Co. Major library wholesalers are also involved in the distribution of microform equipment for libraries.

Problems with Microforms

The proliferation of microform sizes and formats has forced libraries to acquire an array of reading equipment. In addition, libraries face problems of obsolescence of equipment, including inability to obtain replacement parts for existing microform readers which are still in good operating condition because the parts are no longer available from the manufacturer.

There are other drawbacks to increasing the use of microforms at the expense of hard copy. These include the expense of purchasing new equipment to fit the different microform sizes and formats, the fact that some users do not like to use microforms and—a particular problem for libraries hardpressed to maintain adequate staff—the fact that personnel must be available in the microform distribution center at all times.

OUTLOOK FOR MICROFORMS

The BISG forecasts that microforms would grow only slightly less rapidly (92.4%) than total library materials acquisitions (93.4%) between 1976 and 1984. At a time when libraries are concerned about the actual buying power of their acquisition dollars, and also with keeping up with the increasing volume of literature being published, the cost and space advantages of microforms are obvious.

Less certain than the fact that libraries will increase their acquisition of and holdings in microforms is the outcome of conflict between the public and private sectors in micropublishing, which has created what has been termed an "economic-ethical decision on micropublishing" for libraries. The public/private conflict came to a head early in 1978 when John Boyle, then public printer, promised to increase substantially the number of publications the GPO distributes on microfiche to 1350 depository libraries in the U.S. That number rose from 1080 in March 1978 to 5500 by 1979 and to 24,000 in 1980 when about 50% of materials were being distributed in print and the other 50% in fiche. The bulk of the material is comprised of House and Senate bills. Because these publications, which often duplicate private micropublishers' efforts, are free, there is concern among commercial publishers that the GPO action could theoretically force some of them out of the market. In addition, libraries must decide between the economic benefits of receiving publications free of charge for which they previously paid, and facing a situation where the only source of information on the government would be the government itself.

Major titles micropublished by the GPO prior to the acceleration program included *General Accounting Office Reports,* the *Foreign Broadcast Information Service* and the *Joint Publication Research Service.* Publications which have been marketed by the private sector but are micropublished and distributed free to the designated academic libraries by GPO include the *Congressional Record,* all Senate and House bills and other committee hearings. At present 60% of the libraries elect to receive bound copies of the Congressional Record in hard copy versus 40% in fiche.

Overall, however, micropublishing of government information is just one segment of micrographics. Wherever the information comes from, it seems clear that libraries will increase their acquisitions of and holdings in microforms in the early 1980s.

The Library Market for Audiovisual and Other Materials

SUMMARY

Audiovisual sales lagged in the 1970s because of declines in federal funding and constricted budgets in major sales markets. Sales were lower in 1977 than in 1974 and 1975, and still lower by 1979. In the library market, audiovisual expenditures are small and declining, with the 8.5% of acquisitions represented by audiovisual materials in 1976 expected to slip to 5.6% by 1984. Although special and public libraries are expected to increase their share of audiovisual purchases, these libraries nevertheless represent smaller customers.

Audiovisual equipment is sold to libraries through dealers rather than directly by manufacturers, which makes sales trends difficult to pinpoint. Growth is expected to come in the area of nontraditional equipment, such as video and microform hardware.

The library market for furniture and supplies was estimated to be between $50 and $60 million in 1980. It is expected to remain moribund for as long as library budgets remain tight and construction projects are limited.

The library market for book bindings, largely from academic and special libraries, was expected to rise about 22% between 1980 and 1984.

Libraries have turned increasingly to microforms to effect cost and space savings. Over 55 micropublishers were identified in the 1981 *Literary Market Place,* and the micropublishing market was estimated to be around $45 million in 1978.

Microforms are forecast to grow only slightly less rapidly than total library materials acquisitions between 1976 and 1984, as libraries strive to keep up with the increasing volume of literature being published.

FOOTNOTES

1. Alice Harrison Bahr, *Video in Libraries: A Status Report, 1979-80* (White Plains, NY: Knowledge Industry Publications, Inc., 1980).

2. Alice Harrison Bahr, *Microforms: The Librarians' View, 1978-79* (White Plains, NY: Knowledge Industry Publications, Inc., 1978).

8

Summary and Conclusions

As has been suggested elsewhere in this book, the library market in 1984 is likely to look very different from the library market of today.

First, libraries stand on the brink of technological change. They constitute a significant, and still largely untapped, market for the systems described in Chapter 6. Many functions which are currently handled manually are going online in the 1980s, creating initial start-up costs for libraries but thereafter streamlining operations such as circulation, cataloging and security. Computer data bases are proliferating, and computer terminals for reference and for catalog searches are beginning to be used by patrons in major academic and public libraries in the early 1980s and this trend will continue.

Second, basic changes are occuring in the way libraries acquire books and periodicals, again because of the impact of new technology. Online ordering systems instituted by wholesalers and, possibly, publishers speed the delivery of materials and improve libraries' service to patrons.

The new technological environment in libraries demands specially trained individuals, thus extending the professionalism of librarians and their ability to assist patrons. A new type of librarian, the information intermediary, is already becoming common in certain academic and special libraries. If library managers are tough-minded, they will use new technology to improve the productivity of libraries, reversing a trend toward allocating a rising share of the library budget to salaries. But it may take pressure from outside funding agencies to achieve this increase in productivity.

TRADITIONAL LIBRARY ACQUISITIONS IN THE MID-1980s

The changing climate in libraries does not necessarily mean that acquisitions of traditional library materials such as general books, professional and reference books and periodicals will shrink. The market for these publications will depend on the budgetary trends at different kinds of libraries and the way in which librarians perceive the value of each type of publication.

Summary and Conclusions

Because of rising prices of books and periodicals, such as those noted in Chapters 3, 4 and 5, unit sales in the 1980s are expected to show little growth. Book Industry Study Group projections of unit purchases by libraries between 1980 and 1984 suggest that periodical units will decline as much as 14.5% in academic, and 3% in school, libraries. Book acquisitions, on the other hand, are projected to increase anywhere from 11% in school libraries to 16% in academic libraries. Units purchased by special and public libraries are projected to show a rise of 12% and 13% respectively over the four-year period.

This forecast becomes more meaningful when measured by other trends illustrated throughout this report. Essentially, libraries are caught in a squeeze between higher prices for materials and acquisitions budgets which show little increase in real dollars once the impact of inflation is included.

BUDGETARY OUTLOOK FOR LIBRARIES

The outlook for suppliers of publications and systems will depend both on the budget prospects for each class of libraries, and how libraries allocate available dollars among salaries, materials acquisitions and other expenditures. Certainly the overall funding prospects for libraries are mediocre to discouraging in the period 1980 to 1984, for the following reasons:

- Higher education enrollments are expected to peak in the 1980-1982 period and then decline;

- School enrollments will continue to drop over the 1980-1984 period, with federal funds for school libraries and media centers tightly restricted;

- Public libraries face a difficult psychological and economic climate as a result of public resistance to higher state and local taxes, and the fact that libraries traditionally rank far below such essential services as police and fire protection in the scramble for a share of the budget.

Special libraries are an exception to the foregoing analysis. Most of these libraries are in companies, law firms or other organizations that do not depend on public funding. Often their expenditures on information can translate into increased productivity by a professional worker, whether the person is a market research analyst or an engineer working on new product development.

THE SHRINKING LIBRARY DOLLAR

The following sections describe the outlook for library funding, by type of library.

Public Libraries

As indicated in Chapter 2, between 1972-1973, 1976-1977 and 1978-1979, state and local funding for public libraries grew at an annual rate of about 12%, where projections by the Book Industry Study Group peg the average annual growth rate at 9.8%. However, statistics on spending by 10 large public libraries (see Table 2.5) suggest that spending by public libraries on materials was growing only half as fast; i.e, by about 6.3% annually. Thus, during this period, the percentage of public library budgets allocated to materials has dropped from 17.0% in 1972-1973 to 15% in 1977-1978. Knowledge Industry Publications projects total growth in public library spending up to 1983-1984 at nearly 9% per year, suggesting public library expenditures will reach $2.685 billion in 1983-1984.

If public library spending on materials were to level off at 14.0% of the budget, materials acquisitions by public libraries in 1983-1984 would by $376 million, or $34 million above Book Industry Study Group forecasts. Thus, the BISG forecasts may be taken as the low end of a range of forecasts. Table 8.1 illustrates estimated public library spending in this period and shows spending on materials under two assumptions; the BISG assumption, and a more optimistic one.

Academic Libraries

Academic library expenditures grew at an average annual rate of 9.7% between 1970-1971, 1975-1976, and 1976-1977, and are likely to continue

Table 8.1: Estimates of Public Library Spending, 1977-78 to 1983-84

	1977-78	1979-80	1981-82	1983-84
		(millions)		
Total spending	$1600	$1901	$2259	$2685
Spending on				
materials (BISG)	234	252	286	342
As % of total	14.6%	13.3%	12.7%	12.7%
Spending on materials				
as constant %	224	266	316	376
As % of total	14.0%	14.0%	14.0%	14.0%

Source: Knowledge Industry Publications, based on U.S. Bureau of the Census, *Governmental Finances,* 1978-1979; Table 2.3 and Table 2.5.

Summary and Conclusions

to grow at that rate through the early 1980s, given trends in higher education enrollments and expenditures. However, as in public libraries, the budgets are characterized by a shrinking percentage of expenditures allocated to materials. Book Industry Study Group estimates of acquisitions by academic libraries appear to assume a leveling off in the percentage of the budgets allocated to materials, at just under 30%.

Though federal figures for 1977-1978 are not yet available, trends over the last few years indicate that the percentage of academic library budgets allocated to materials may already be well under 30%. Academic library statistics (see Table 2.2) indicate the figure has dropped to 25%. Therefore, Table 8.2 gives two alternate sets of assumptions; one showing spending on materials at a constant 25%, the other illustrating materials sales if the percentage should continue to shrink. In this case, the BISG forecasts would seem to be on the optimistic side of the possible ranges of materials sales. Should the percentage of budgets going for materials continue to drop at the same rate as in recent years, the BISG forecasts could be high by as much as $139 million in 1983-1984.

Table 8.2: Estimates of Academic Library Spending, 1977-78 to 1983-84

	1977-78	1979-80	1981-82	1983-84
		(millions)		
Total expenditures	$1386	$1678	$2031	$2457
Spending on materials (BISG)	435	490	589	680
As % of total	31.4%	29.2%	29.0%	27.7%
Spending on materials a constant %	347	420	508	614
As % of total	25.0%	25.0%	25.0%	25.0%
Spending on materials, as declining %	347	403	467	541
As % of total	25.0%	24.0%	23.0%	22.0%

Source: Knowledge Industry Publications projections, based on Tables 2.10, 2.11, 2.12.

School Libraries

Declining enrollments became a fact of life for companies selling to elementary and high schools in 1972, after el-hi enrollment peaked at 51.5 million in 1971. El-hi enrollments declined 5% between 1974 and 1978, and were expected to drop another 7% between 1979 and 1983.

At the same time, federal funding for school libraries and media centers became tighter. Retrenchment began in the form of consolidation of facilities, taxpayers' resistance to educational costs and higher

THE SHRINKING LIBRARY DOLLAR

teachers' salaries. The result was fewer dollars to operate school libraries, and a corresponding decline in acquisition dollars to buy the materials school libraries used to build collections in the late 1960s and early 1970s.

It is difficult to project school library materials acquisitions in the 1980s because the last year for which expenditures for these libraries were available is 1978 (see Table 2.14). In that year, materials acquisitions (books, periodicals, audiovisuals) totaled $271 million, or about 20.0% of total expenditures.

Projecting an increase of about 1% annually in total expenditures, and assuming materials expenditures remain constant at 20.0%, school libraries would have spent $271 million in 1977-1978 on materials, a figure that would rise to $294 million in 1983-1984.

These projections would mean $178 million less in school library purchases than the forecast of the Book Industry Study Group, as illustrated in Table 8.3.

Table 8.3: Estimates of School Library Spending, 1977-78 to 1983-84

	1977-78	1979-80	1981-82	1983-84
		(millions)		
Total Expenditures	$1385	$1413	$1441	$1470
Spending on materials (BISG)	331	371	412	472
As % of total	23.9%	26.3%	28.6%	32.1%
Spending on materials as constant %	271	283	288	294
As % of total	20.0%	20.0%	20.0%	20.0%
Spending on materials, as declining %	263	254	245	235
As % of total	19.0%	18.0%	17.0%	16.0%

Source: Knowledge Industry Publications, based on Table 2.14 and 2.16.

Using another set of assumptions, or a declining percentage of total expenditures going to materials, the figures would decline from $263 million to $235 million in this period.

Special Libraries

Special libraries, today the largest segment of the U.S. library market, constitute the best growth opportunity, particularly for publishers of professional books and journals. These libraries and information centers are insulated from the ups and downs of public funding, and are often able to pass on to an internal department or to an outside customer the

Summary and Conclusions

cost of information, whether the information is a book or a computer search.

Unfortunately, the total amount of money spent by special libraries (including government libraries) is difficult to estimate. Table 8.4 uses the figure for special library expenditures form Table 1.1 and projects it forward using the assumption of 11% annual growth. Book Industry Study Group forecasts of materials acquisitions are compared to alternative estimates, based on a constant 30% of special library budgets allocated to materials.

TOTAL MARKET IN 1984

The estimate for total library market acquisitions of publications and systems can be seen in Table 8.5. The year 1984 is selected in order to have the benefit of BISG projections and to compare them with alternative estimates, which are in some cases more conservative, in other cases more optimistic. Revenues from systems are estimated to grow, conservatively, at 25% per year, and optimistically, at 40% per year. Revenues from supplies, equipment and other are estimated to grow, conservatively, at 5% a year, and optimistically, at 10% per year.

IMPLICATIONS OF LIBRARY TRENDS FOR LIBRARIES AND LIBRARIANS

The overall trends have different implications for different types of libraries. The following sections address the major points by type of library.

Table 8.4: Estimates of Special Library Spending, 1978-84

	1978	1980	1982	1984
		(millions)		
Total spending	$1300	$1602	$1973	$2432
Spending on				
materials (BISG)	376	501	609	710
As % of total	28.9%	31.3%	30.9%	29.2%
Spending on materials				
as constant %	390	481	592	730
As % of total	30.0%	30.0%	30.0%	30.0%

Source: Knowledge Industry Publications estimates; Book Industry Study Group.

THE SHRINKING LIBRARY DOLLAR

Table 8.5: Estimates of Total Library Market, 1980 and 1984

Publications by Sector	1980 Conservative	1980 Optimistic	1984 Conservative	1984 Optimistic
		(millions)		
Public	$ 252	$ 266	$ 342	$ 376
Academic	403	490	541	680
School	254	371	235	472
Special	481	501	710	730
Total publications	$1390	$1628	$1828	$2258
Total systems	135	135	330	519
Total other	50	50	72	81
Grand total	$1575	$1813	$2230	$2858

Source: Knowledge Industry Publications, Inc.

Public Libraries

Americans are generally pleased with their public libraries. However, many are unclear that the principal support of public library funding is local government; thus it behooves libraries and interested citizens to get this message across. Furnishing enhanced reference services, by telephone, through wider interlibrary loan and even via computer, would strengthen the position of libraries, as would offering educational and employment assistance. Libraries are also urged to become the principal resource of community information in their localities. The fact that such services are available must be more effectively publicized.

Staffing by professional librarians in public libraries has increased more than expected. Attendance at continuing education courses offered by library associations is on the rise and recommended to meet the challenge of the possible changing role of libraries.

Public libraries generally spend over half of their budgets on salaries and wages, with supplies and materials the next largest category. Here, books account for close to 80% of the total. However, large libraries serving important segments of the public are often spending a declining percentage of total expenditures on materials. Libraries are urged to pay strict attention to these percentages and to make the adherence to certain percentages a matter of library policy subject to public knowledge and review.

Libraries serving larger populations may do well to continue the

Summary and Conclusions

perceived trend of offsetting a decline in local funding through increases in private as well as state dollars.

Academic Libraries

Academic libraries vary widely in terms of collections and expenditures as well as in terms of functions served. The dramatic rise in the number of college students and federal funding programs which helped spur library materials purchase in the 1970s have fallen victim to a declining birth rate and a call for less government spending in the late 1970s and early 1980s. Moreover, rising costs of materials and personnel have continued to erode the capabilities of academic libraries to build collections and provide services. Professional staff in these libraries has also declined.

The 1980 election of Ronald Reagan has put even the small amount of federal dollars that are provided for academic library materials (Higher Education Act II-A funds for college library resources) into jeopardy. Fortunately, the special needs of research libraries and their existence as a national resource continue to be recognized and the newer funding (Higher Education Act II-D funds for research libraries) has so far emerged unscathed from the federal budget paring process.

The incipient shift of dollars from book to periodical purchases has not occurred, according to both Book Industry Study Group and Association of Research Libraries Group statistics. Since this expected dramatic shift was highly publicized, informed library policies may well have reversed the trend. Thus, collection balance may be a function of informed management. Moreover, concerned alumni groups can help their alma maters compete for the decreasing pool of college applicants by ensuring that the library maintains its standing.

Academic libraries are finding that investment in electronic book theft and security systems can pay for itself in a few years by stemming losses of costly materials. In their struggle, academic libraries are also looking to cooperatives for assistance, as witnessed by the growth of the Research Libraries Group and other library cooperatives in recent years.

School Libraries

Full time equivalent staff in school library and media centers has decreased along with student enrollments. With the birth rate remaining low, costs of materials continuing to rise and taxpayer resistance unabated, this depressed state is expected to continue. The purchase of audiovisual materials will continue to decline.

THE SHRINKING LIBRARY DOLLAR

In an effort to decrease costs, schools have increased their reliance on purchases through jobbers. Personal student membership in book clubs as well as greater cooperation between school and local public libraries are other methods schools have used with good results.

Special Libraries

Although statistics are hard to obtain for special libraries, the special library is the true growth area for libraries and librarians. The membership of the Special Libraries Association is at an all-time high of close to 11,487, as reported by executive director David Bender at the association's 1981 annual conference.

Both book and periodical acquisitions are expected to gain in dollars and unit purchases. Special libraries have replaced academic libraries as the largest purchasers of microforms. In fact, acquisitions by special libraries are expected to show significant gains in every category. Special libraries are also good customers for online data bases since searching can often be paid for from a company research budget. In commerce, industry, law and medicine—where special libraries are situated—information and knowledge are recognized as having a real and often competitive value.

CONCLUSIONS FOR LIBRARIES AND LIBRARIANS

Those entering the library field should consider the growth area of the profession the special library and information center. Established librarians are advised to seek out continuing education courses, both for personal growth and career advantage at a time when libraries stand at the threshold of technological change.

Careful attention to balance and percentages of expenditures going for materials can help both public and academic libraries maintain their collections. Both types of libraries should make sure their constituencies are aware of what the shrinking library dollar is doing to resources in order to elicit greater support. Public and academic libraries may be seeking more funding from private sources as public funds dwindle. Public libraries might also give more serious consideration to the controversial question of charging modest fees for unusual and costly services such as online searching.

Although there seemed little hope of increased funding or enrollments for school libraries, as this report was being completed, there were signs that inflation might be abating. If true, the purchasing power of these and all libraries would be increased.

Summary and Conclusions

IMPLICATIONS OF LIBRARY TRENDS FOR PUBLISHERS AND SYSTEMS SUPPLIERS

The overall economic trends in library budgets and expenditures also have varied implications for the different types of publishers and suppliers of other library services. The following sections sketch the major points by type of supplier, and should be of interest to libraries as well.

General Book Publishers, Adult and Juvenile

School libraries constitute the largest library market for general books followed by public libraries. Academic and special libraries are smaller customers for general books. All types of libraries are forecast to increase purchases of general books between 1978 and 1984.

The dollar sales will translate into modest increases in unit sales in the adult trade category. Mass market unit sales are predicted to show somewhat greater strength, while unit sales of juvenile hardbounds, a small category, should outpace those of paperbound books.

The number of retail book outlets has expanded greatly through the growth of chains like Walden Book Co. and B. Dalton, thus putting books within the reach of more consumers than ever before.

A substantial portion of the revenue increases generated by general books has come from price increases. Mass market fiction titles rose 89.7% in price from 1978 to 1980.

For book publishers in general, there is less opportunity in institutional and formal education markets (el-hi and college) but much more opportunity in the consumer market, since there are now millions of college-educated adults with a predisposition to books.

The library market is important for juvenile books, with about 70% of sales generated in that market. Many juvenile publishers derive the bulk of their sales from the library market. Juvenile books sold to the library market are heavily dependent on reviews and book awards for sales.

Professional Book Publishers

Professional book publishers must be divided into two categories inorder to assess the implications of library trends.

The first category, consisting of publishers of sci/tech books and scholarly books, like Wiley, Plenum and Van Nostrand Reinhold, are threatened by current trends in library expenditures and in spending patterns. A relatively high percentage of their sales is to academic libraries where book budgets are under pressure.

Publishers of business and other professional books and services, like Prentice-Hall, McGraw-Hill and Commerce Clearing House, have better opportunities. Not only are special libraries the healthiest segment of the library market at present, but these publishers have only begun to exploit sales prospects among individual business executives and other professionals. Moreover, the retail market should continue to grow along with the growth in full-line and better financed bookstores.

Periodical Publishers

Publishers of general consumer magazines like *Time* and *Reader's Digest* already depend very little on the library market, and will depend less so as they continue to increase single copy and subscription prices to individual consumers.

Publishers of scholarly journals, on the other hand, like Pergamon and Williams & Wilkins, have few real alternatives to the library market. As library budgets have failed to keep pace with inflation in recent years, and as libraries have devoted a declining portion of the budget to materials, these publishers have pushed up subscription prices rapidly in order to keep revenues growing. In the short-term this price inflation has resulted in the diversion of book funds to periodicals, in academic and special library budgets. But as libraries get more serious about resource sharing, and as they increase their volume of photocopying in reaction to higher journal prices, the effect on journal publishers will inevitably be to slow, or to stop entirely, growth in revenues and profits.

Journal publishers also have both the most to fear and the most to gain from the advent of computer technology into information dissemination. Many printed abstract journals face the prospect of replacement entirely by online, on-demand services that choose for the researcher just those articles in which he is interested. Primary journals will continue to exist, but the challenge to their publishers is to be able to sell their information in the form of separates (reprints or off-prints of individual articles), to store the full text of articles in data bases that can be accessed as needed or to get appropriate compensation when their material is photocopied. Some moves have and are being made in these directions through the Copyright Clearance Center and publisher law suits in the U.S., and a consortium of scientific technical publishers in the U.K.

Systems Companies

Companies supplying computer-based systems for cataloging, processing, reference, circulation control and other tasks appear to have excellent near-term prospects in the library market. Because the library market is miniscule to a Digital Equipment Corp. these companies have not developed products specifically for it, leaving the way clear for small firms like CL Systems to buy off-the-shelf computer gear and tailor it to the library environment.

With the exception of online reference searching, library automation is still limited to housekeeping, recordkeeping activities that have only minor impact on the end user. However, as computer storage and telecommunications costs continue to drop, there will be opportunities to personalize the dissemination of information. This will mean more information terminals in the library for patrons, or, as an alternative, more information terminals in the office, research lab or living room that will enable the individual to bypass libraries entirely. Organizations like OCLC, the New York Times Information Service and Dialog Information Service undoubtedly recognize that just because their service is often delivered to a library reference department today, this does not mean the same pattern will prevail into the 1980s.

LIBRARY ECONOMICS AND MATERIALS BUDGETS

A problem that no supplier of information to libraries can afford to ignore is the trend—well documented in this report—for libraries to allocate an ever shrinking percentage of their budgets for materials. Whether this trend results from poor management in libraries, or whether shifting money from materials to personnel actually results in better service to patrons, cannot be determined from statistics alone. But it would be of obvious benefit to publishers and libraries alike to sponsor comparative studies in the economics of library budget management, to assess how institutions of similar size and budgets differ in their allocation of resources. Along the same vein, it will serve no purpose for libraries to embark on automation programs involving the most sophisticated computer hardware and programs, if the end result is to keep reducing the acquisitions of books, periodicals and other resources that have traditionally been the foundation of library service.

CONCLUSIONS FOR PUBLISHERS AND SYSTEM SUPPLIERS

The library market is not a glamorous one, nor is it, on the evidence presented in this report, a market that is growing much. But libraries are an essential part of American cultural and educational life; they remain vital to academic research, to public awareness and enlightenment and to the dissemination of information. Many publishers of general books depend on libraries for a portion of sales and profits; most publishers of specialized books and periodicals depend on libraries for their economic existence. As the trends highlighted in this report indicate, library suppliers will have to demonstrate special skill and foresight to deal with trends in this market over the next five years.

Appendix: Profiles

Profiles

Baker & Taylor Companies
Bibliographic Retrieval Services
Blackwell North America, Inc.
Brodart Industries
R.R. Bowker Co.
CL Systems, Inc.
Commerce Clearing House, Inc.
Dialog Information Services, Inc.
F.W. Faxon Co., Inc.
Gaylord Bros., Inc.
Grolier Inc.
Grosset & Dunlap, Inc.
Harcourt Brace Jovanovich
Harper & Row
Moore-Cottrell Subscription Services, Inc.
OCLC (Online Computer Library Center)
Plenum Publishing Corp.
Prentice-Hall, Inc.
System Development Corp.
University Microfilms International
John Wiley & Sons, Inc.
The H.W. Wilson Co.

9

Profiles

Baker & Taylor Companies
(division of W.R. Grace & Co.)
1515 Broadway
New York, NY 10036
(212) 730-7650

Baker & Taylor (B&T), which calls itself the librarian's library, is the largest wholesaler of books to libraries in the U.S. With an estimated 80% of its volume derived from institutional (library) sales, it is more than twice the size of its closest competitor, Brodart. Baker & Taylor sees a constricting institutional marketplace, and has therefore diversified, with some success, into the bookstore market to insure growth. The remaining 20% of sales are to retail bookstores. Approximately 5% of B&T's revenues are estimated to come from foreign sources. A well-established name in the library market, Baker & Taylor has relied on aggressiveness in services and discount practices to penetrate the bookstore market and has plans for continued expansion in that area.

Baker & Taylor discounts are a minimum of 33% off list price for school and public libraries, 30% for academic libraries. Its closest competitors include Brodart in the school and public library markets and Blackwell North America in the academic market. Other competition in the school and library markets comes from Josten's, and regional wholesalers provide competition in all three markets. In October 1978, Baker & Taylor acquired the hardcover inventory of Demco, a school and public library wholesaler.

In addition to direct order business, Baker & Taylor offers a host of auxiliary services such as cataloging and processing, a continuation service and an approval plan. The company markets a variety of automated services for libraries under the trade name LIBRIS. These include BATAB (Baker & Taylor's Automated Buying system), machine-readable catalog records and conversion of card catalogs to COM.

Although it maintains a nominal audiovisual software distribution, by 1978 Baker & Taylor was de-emphasizing this area of business. Widely advertised prior to the mid-1970s, the audiovisual component at one time claimed to distribute media from 700 producers. Its potential was never fulfilled because it could not supply products from some of the major audiovisual firms, including Society for Visual Education (Singer) and Encyclopaedia Britannica Educational Corp.

Each of the company's four regional warehouses has a sales manager and a sales force. Baker & Taylor's total nationwide sales force numbers approximately 60.

Although wholesalers are traditionally engaged in a "thin" margin business, Baker & Taylor insists it has achieved some economies of operation and says it makes a "satisfactory profit." Future growth will depend upon various company efforts currently underway to improve profitability, including a $10 million modernization program. It expects that the result will be service improvements to both the library and bookstore customers.

Bibliographic Retrieval Services
Corporation Park, Building 702
Scotia, NY 12302
(518) 374-5011

Bibliographic Retrieval Services entered the online computer-based bibliographic data service market in January 1977, challenging the two established vendors in that market, Lockheed and System Development Corp. The company was started by its two top executives, who had been on the faculty of the State University of New York (SUNY). The new data company began operation offering access to about a dozen data bases popular with academic libraries, including agriculture, biology, business, chemistry, computer science, management education, engineering, medicine, physics and psychology.

By the end of 1978, BRS was offering access to 22 data bases. Additional files included Social Science Citation Index, drug abuse and alcohol use/abuse, environmental impact and NIMIS (instructional materials for the handicapped). Later additions included the National Institute of Mental Health file and the Smithsonian Science Information file. Data base selection is done by committee. By 1981, BRS had approximately 40 publicly available data bases.

BRS's main challenge to Lockheed and SDC was in the area of fees, with BRS emerging as a low cost competitor, claiming it would offer savings of more than 50% to heavy users.

THE SHRINKING LIBRARY DOLLAR

BRS bases its fee structure on annual subscriptions. Typical fees are as follows: $750 for 25 connect hours per year, $1500 for 60 hours, $2400 for 120 hours and $3800 for 240 hours. Per hour charges drop as hours increase.

BRS quickly attracted some 150 charter subscribers, more than one third of them in the medical field. A major appeal of BRS to medical institutions was access to the MEDLARS data base, which no other commercial distributor offered. This enabled BRS to take hold quickly as a distributor. About 2000 institutions currently use BRS.

BRS's rapid growth made it an attractive takeover target. On October 16, 1980, Thyssen-Bornemisza-NV, an international holding company, acquired BRS for a reputed $9 million through its U.S. subsidiary, Indian Head. The company said BRS would function as an independent operating unit of Indian Head's "flagship" company, Information Handling Services. The company also acquired Predicasts, Capital Information Services and several other European online information organizations.

Blackwell North America, Inc.
(subsidiary of Blackwell's Delaware Inc.)
10300 S.W. Allen Blvd.
Beaverton, OR 97005
(503) 643-8423

Blackwell North America was formed in January 1975 by B.H. Blackwell of Oxford, England, a publisher and bookseller. Blackwell acquired the assets of financially troubled Richard Abel & Co. for $1.2 million. The new company, Blackwell North America, subsequently sold International Scholarly Book Services, a subsidiary, to Richard Abel.

Blackwell North America is a major book wholesaler to the academic library market, for which it also provides a full array of cataloging and bibliographic services, computer based and otherwise. The company says that 99.5% of its sales are to the library market. It serves Australia, the United Kingdom, Europe and the Middle East as well as the U.S. The company has close to 250 employees, about half of whom work in the Oregon headquarters. Blackwell also has an eastern regional office in Blackwood, NJ.

Since its inception, Blackwell North America has suffered some ups and downs. Net worth showed a dramatic drop between 1975 and 1976, when the company switched from Abel to Blackwell ownership, as a

Profiles

result of operating losses, writeoffs and chargeoffs of discontinued ordering system designed for 24-hour turnaround. Brodart also opened a Secaucus, NJ facility, challenging bookstore wholesalers in the New operations. (Writeoffs comprised about half the loss.) Sales for 1980 increased 23.8% from 1978, and operations for the period were profitable, according to the company. The company estimated that 1981 sales would total $30 million.

Blackwell's main competitors in the academic library market are Baker & Taylor, Midwest and Ballen. It considers itself number two to Baker & Taylor in terms of academic library market share, and admits its own growth will have to come from increasing market share. Despite the fact that libraries' materials budgets buy less every year, Blackwell says this decline in purchasing power has affected it only at the community college level, and believes that its own academic libraries are more immune to the cutbacks.

Brodart Industries
1609 Memorial Ave.
Williamsport, PA 17701
(717) 326-2461

Brodart, founded in 1939, calls itself The Library Company. It is the second largest wholesaler of books to libraries in the U.S. In addition, Brodart wholesales records and cassettes to libraries, sells supplies and equipment to libraries and has retail bookstores in six California locations as well as in Williamsport, PA. During the 1970s, Brodart invested heavily in expenditures for library and bookstore automation, a move which may help its performance in the long-term but kept earnings relatively flat in 1976, 1977 and 1978. Brodart is strongly committed to library automation.

Among its innovations was the Instant Response Ordering System (IROS), an online computerized system that permits librarians to communicate directly with Brodart's centralized computer to get information on titles and to place orders.

IROS was replaced by OLAS, the On Line Acquisitions System, a fully developed and completely operational online book ordering system. Brodart claims 180 OLAS systems are up and running in all types of libraries; special, public and academic.

In addition, Brodart introduced Book Express in 1978, an online book ordering system designed for 24-hour turnaround. Brodart also opened a Secaucus, NJ facility, challenging bookstore wholesalers in the New

THE SHRINKING LIBRARY DOLLAR

York metropolitan area. The company said it would stress "next day delivery and breadth of inventory;" its move put it in direct competition for bookstore orders with Baker & Taylor and Bookazine. Brodart also ships library books through the Secaucus operation, but no library services are offered through this facility.

Brodart manufactures 55% of the library supplies and equipment that it sells, ranging from tape and glue to card catalog cabinets and circulation control systems. About one-third of its business comes from competitive bids to large public library systems and school districts. The company has about 30 salesmen and technical representatives who call on libraries.

Brodart gives discounts off list price to libraries depending on the buying power of the institution. Many discounts are negotiated and may reflect different kinds of services.

Brodart's book inventory exceeds 1.5 million volumes covering approximately 100,000 titles at any given time, although 200,000 titles may be handled over the course of a year. The company's main warehouse is in Williamsport, PA; smaller inventory centers are located in City of Industry, CA; Brantford, Ontario and the new Secaucus, NJ facility. Its major manufacturing facility is also located in Williamsport, PA.

Because Brodart strives to sell a service with its books, it offers a full line of cataloging and processing services for libraries. These include a collection access system that transfers a library's card catalog onto microfilm, which is updated periodically. In 1976, Brodart acquired the assets of INOVAR Corp., a company that produced both book and microform catalogs for libraries.

Brodart's MacNaughton book leasing plan makes popular titles available to libraries for periods when they are in high demand. A certain number of new books are selected each month and a like number of previously selected books which are no longer in demand are returned.

Brodart acquired H.R. Huntting in late 1978 to enhance its position in the school library market. In a larger sense, the acquisition was also evidence of the difficulty which smaller wholesalers are having in remaining viable in the school library market.

Brodart acquired Dimondstein Book Co., Inc. in December 1978, and Josten's Library Services, Inc. in March 1979. On September 29, 1980, Brodart purchased 27 additional J.K. Gill retail bookstores on the West Coast, for a total of 42 outlets.

Profiles

R.R. Bowker Co.
(subsidiary of Xerox Corp.)
1180 Avenue of the Americas
New York, NY 10036
(212) 764-5100

Bowker was established in 1872 as The Bowker Co. and incorporated as R.R. Bowker Co. in 1914. Xerox acquired it in 1967. It is now part of the $215 million Xerox publishing operation, which also includes Ginn & Co., an elementary and secondary textbook publisher; Xerox Education Publications, classroom newspapers and periodicals, book clubs and multimedia materials; and University Microfilms. R.R. Bowker Co. consists of three divisions, magazine, book and data base, all of which are heavily involved in the library market.

The magazine division's flagship publication is *Publishers Weekly,* which has 13,000 libraries among its 33,000 subscribers. The magazine division is heavily dependent upon *Publishers Weekly,* although several of its other components also do well, including the semimonthly *Library Journal* and the monthly (during the school year) *School Library Journal.* The latter two were once a single magazine, but since their split in the mid-1970s, the latter has attracted even more subscribers than *Library Journal. School Library Journal*'s subscriptions number 41,000, while *Library Journal* has 31,000 subscribers. Other R.R. Bowker periodicals include *LJ-SLJ Hotline,* actually a weekly newsletter which covers news and developments affecting librarians, their services and patrons, and *Weekly Record,* recording American book production. Monthly and bimonthly publications include *American Book Publishing Record, Forthcoming Books* and *Subject Guide to Forthcoming Books.* Another monthly, *Bookviews,* was halted following its December 1978 issue. It had a short life span, having been launched in September 1977. *Previews,* a magazine for audiovisual software reviews, which had a variety of difficulties, including lagging advertising sales, was incorporated into *School Library Journal.*

Bowker's data services division, considered to be the component of the company which prompted its purchase by Xerox, publishes *Books in Print* (BIP), which sells some 40,000 copies annually in the U.S. and another 5000 abroad. BIP is considered to be highly profitable, and has many related titles: *Children's Books in Print, El-Hi Textbooks in Print,* etc. Two other major products are *Ulrich's International Periodicals Directory* and *Ulrich's Quarterly,* which have heavy sales outside the U.S. They are sold 100% by direct mail.

THE SHRINKING LIBRARY DOLLAR

Bowker's book division publishes *Publishers Trade List Annual,* a multivolume compilation of the lists of American book publishers and foreign publishers with American distributors. *PTLA* is believed to make money on advertising but has incurred lower unit sales in the late 1970s. The book division also publishes the marketplace publications, including *Literary Market Place, International Literary Market Place,* etc. Other publications are institutional directories and biographical directories, such as *American Library Directory Updating Service* and *American Men and Women of Science.* These are compiled and edited by Jacques Cattell Press.

Three of R.R. Bowker's standard and widely used directories *American Men and Women of Science, Ulrich's International Periodicals Directory* and the massive *Books in Print* became publicly available for online searching via Bibliographic Retrieval Services' on-line search system in 1981. The data bases had been in test mode since 1979.

Other Bowker operations include its profitable mailing lists, over 40 of them to libraries, and IRIS, Bowker's International Rights Information Service which was once offered as a separate service but was incorporated into one edition of *Publishers Weekly* per month in January 1979. Unipub, a division of Bowker, distributes international publications such as those of UNESCO.

For the future, the clearest direction for Bowker to follow would seem to be the expansion of its data services division, which offers many prospects for growth. (There are drawbacks, however, since Bowker faces stiff competition from others entrenched in that market, including wholesalers like Baker & Taylor, Brodart and Ingram as well as OCLC, Inc.) Xerox Publishing has identified professional, reference and technical books as well as information products and services and book clubs as areas in which it can achieve growth. Bowker is certainly well positioned to help it achieve its growth in several of these categories.

CL Systems, Inc.
81 Norwood Ave.
Newtonville, MA 02160
(617) 965-6310

CL Systems, marketer of the LIBS 100 automated circulation system, is the largest purveyor of such systems in the library market. It was organized in 1967 as Computer Library Services. Assets of the original company were sold at auction in June 1976, and CL Systems, Inc., a new company financed by the management team that was running Computer Library Services, emerged as the only bidder at the auction. The infusion of capital which came following the auction allowed CL Systems to speed up its development program.

The LIBS 100 is in an online system based on a minicomputer and utilizing a light pen device to scan bar-coded labels affixed to both books and library patron identification cards. On the market since 1972, it claimed 292 installations at the end of April 1981. It offers a number of capabilities, including circulation control and a special process called REQUEST which handles the searching, notice generation and routing of books that occur when a book is not immediately on the shelf. Other capabilities include accumulating and printing circulation statistics as well as other statistical reports, locating and retrieving books requested for the future. In early 1981, CL announced a multiprocessing capability so its circulation system could serve the needs of very large libraries. The company also has plans for a low cost system for libraries with annual circulation of around 200,000.

CL Systems has a variety of financing arrangements for its LIBS 100, which include outright purchase plus a monthly maintenance charge and lease purchase plans that let customers spread the cost over a number of years. The bulk of its leases receivable are assigned to an independent leasing company. Its financial statement for fiscal 1978 indicated that it had $1.3 million of sales and $802,454 of gross profit related to sales-type leases. Those numbers were up from $186,200 of sales and $111,600 in fiscal 1977. However, CL had only $141,000 of sales and $91,239 of related gross profit in 1980, and similar amounts for 1979 were $305,900 and $178,908 respectively.

CL systems has been an aggressive presence in the automated circulation system marketplace, so much so that a competitor, DataPhase, filed suit against CL in June 1978 alleging antitrust claims for monopolization of the market, predatory pricing tactics, state law claims for disparagement of the plaintiff and its products and unfair competition. DataPhase sought injunctive relief and punitive damages of over $8 million. CL Systems characterized the suit as a "sour grapes lawsuit." The suit was settled out of court in spring 1981, without prejudice to the issues being refiled. Under the terms of the settlement, CL agreed to be responsible for the costs of a recently completed appeal.

Whatever its competitors think of CL Systems, its position as the leading marketer of automated circulation systems was more than secure at the end of 1980, and its prospects for growth were encouraging. The company anticipated that sales would total $14 million in 1981, up from

THE SHRINKING LIBRARY DOLLAR

$11.7 million in 1980. Its systems are attractive in the library market for a number of reasons, not the least of which is the fact that CLSI's large number of installations gives future customers confidence in its ability to provide service and to further improve its system.

Commerce Clearing House, Inc.
4025 W. Peterson Ave.
Chicago, IL 60646
(312) 583-8500

More than two-thirds of Commerce Clearing House's revenues, and the bulk of its revenue from continuing operations, is derived from publishing activities. It publishes current information primarily in the fields of tax and business law and offers other publications and services in areas of allied interest. CCH's principal format for publishing is looseleaf reports, offered on an annual subscription basis, and devoted to subject matter within specified areas. These include federal taxes, labor, securities-finance, state taxes, insurance, social security, legislation, business and others.

Complementing these reports are books, booklets and casebooks on subjects germane to the reports. CCH has its own printing and mailing facilities to expedite distribution of its publications.

Libraries are an important market for CCH publications, as are lawyers, accountants and other professional consultants as well as business organizations, schools and governmental agencies. CCH has a direct selling organization of some 482 sales representatives, with parallel sales promotion made by direct mail.

A subsidiary company, Facts on File, Inc., publishes current issues summarizing news events and reproducing editorials appearing in U.S. newspapers. Libraries and schools constitute the major markets for Facts on File publications.

Part of the increased revenue recognized in the last two years is due to the new looseleaf subscription products and books, including the acquisition of the Quebec-based French language publisher Formules Municipales L'teé in 1979. The balance of the revenue increase is due to additional sales of existing products and the cumulative effect of price increases in 1980 and prior years.

Interest in tax and financial concerns by individuals and institutions should place CCH in a strong position to continue to increase publishing sales, including those to libraries, in the 1980s.

Dialog Information Services, Inc.
(a subsidiary of Lockheed Corp.)
3460 Hillview Ave.
Palo Alto, CA 94304
(415) 858-2700

Lockheed's Dialog Information Retrieval Service, which competes with System Development Corp. and Bibliographic Retrieval Services, dates to the mid-1960s, when Lockheed began working with files from National Aeronautics and Space Administration (NASA) and the Atomic Energy Commission's Nuclear Science Abstracts. As of May 1980, Dialog provided access to more than 120 data bases on subjects that included engineering, geology, education, electronics, agriculture, physics, chemistry, psychology, social sciences, computers and control, business, patents, federally sponsored research and many others. Lockheed's plans call for adding new data bases constantly. It recently announced that it would make all of the cataloging of the Library of Congress available for online searching through LC MARC tapes and an exclusive contract with Carrollton Press, Inc. for the REMARC data base.

Lockheed bases its fee structure on computer connect hours, with the hourly fee ranging from $15 to $150 to $300 depending on which data base is searched. In early 1981 only one data base, CLAIMS/UNITERM from IFI/Plenum, cost $300; the next most expensive was SCISEARCH at $130 with the vast majority of files well under $100. The average price excluding those files is approximately $55 to $65. Like System Development Corp., Lockheed offers discounts of between $5 and $15 per connect hour according to volume of usage. Dialog had some 13,000 customers by 1981.

In addition to Dialog, Lockheed Information Systems was involved for three years in a National Science Foundation-funded experiment called DIALIB, which explored the relationship between cost and demand for online services at public libraries. According to the ensuing report, there is a public library market for online services, and small business employees, college students, local government officials and selected other public library patrons can provide enough demand to make online data base retrieval a viable venture for public libraries.

Dialog Information Services, which will soon have more of MEDLINE available than the National Library of Medicine (1966 files to date), was reorganized as a subsidiary of Lockheed Corp. in spring 1981. The move reflected a need for more autonomy and greater flexibility. Dialog had been a division of Lockheed Missiles and Space Co. which concentrates on government contracts and aerospace.

THE SHRINKING LIBRARY DOLLAR

F.W. Faxon Co., Inc.
15 Southwest Park
Westwood, MA 02090
(617) 329-3350

Faxon, founded in 1881, is a library subscription agency, providing periodicals, serials, annuals and continuations for libraries throughout the world.

It also has a small publishing division which publishes a series of indexes known as "The Useful Reference Series of Library Books" on various topics. Subject matter and number of indexes published per year vary; the list included 120 titles at the end of 1980.

A Faxon subsidiary, The Combined Book Exhibit, Inc. (Hawthorne, NY), acquired in 1976, exhibits books and magazines for publishers at library shows such as the American Library Association meetings.

Faxon said revenues were $123.0 million in fiscal 1981, making it substantially larger than many of the companies whose products it provides. It is one of the largest and oldest of more than 200 companies which compete in the magazine subscription agency field.

Gaylord Bros., Inc.
PO Box 61
Syracuse, NY 13201
(315) 457-5070

Gaylord Bros. sells supplies, equipment, systems and publications to the library market. The company, which dates back to the early 1900s, is considered the leader in the library supplies and equipment field (see Chapter 7). Its products include catalog cards, plastic bookcovers, mending tape and binders in the supply field and specialized cabinets and index/reference tables, among other items, in the furniture field. It has a furniture manufacturing division located in Sanford, NC.

In the publications field, an area which Gaylord entered in the mid-1970s, Gaylord has published *Artists Market, Access, Children's Media Market, Directory of Schools* and *Librarian's Handbook*. Gaylord also competes in the systems market. In the circulation system market, Gaylord distributes the Gaylord Automated Circulation Control System, a product of its Library Systems division. It had 10 installations plus one demonstration site at the end of 1978. Gaylord also had several dozen electronic security system installations at the close of 1978, giving it ground floor strength in both of these systems markets.

The company's outlook for the 1980s should be aided by its newer areas of business, namely publications and systems. Although the library market for furniture and equipment is likely to remain moribund in the early 1980s, Gaylord is already an established name in the systems market. In addition, its position as a leader in the supplies and equipment market gives it an inherent advantage over some of its smaller competitors.

Grolier Inc.
Old Sherman Turnpike
Danbury, CT 06816
(203) 797-3500

Grolier incurred five years of financial difficulties in the 1970s, which culminated with a debt restructuring plan completed in December 1977. Between 1973 and 1977, the company's sales declined 26.8%, partially from a planned sales reduction and also from the shutdown of certain foreign operations. Grolier has incurred heavy foreign exchange losses, particularly in the Swiss franc, Canadian dollar and Mexican peso. A sales slowdown was felt in all phases of Grolier operations, as a poor funding picture in public and school libraries compounded Grolier's other problems. However, Grolier experienced its third year of profitability in 1979. Net income increased from $3 million in 1979 to $9.3 million in 1980. The improvement in earnings was attributable to favorable foreign exchange results, as compared to 1979 and prior years.

Grolier sells its encyclopedias to the library market by more than 100 salespeople who make direct calls on libraries. Best known among its line of multivolume reference works are *The New Book of Knowledge*, a 20-volume curriculum-oriented encyclopedia edited especially for children in the elementary grades, and the *Encyclopedia Americana*, a 30-volume reference work on popular and technical subjects edited for secondary school and college students. Other encyclopedias include *Encyclopedia International*, a 20-volume work edited for school and home use; *The Book of Popular Science, Lands and Peoples;* and *The Book of Art*. International editions, such as *The Australian Encyclopedia* and *El Mundo Pintoresco*, a Spanish-language translation and adaptation of *Lands and Peoples,* are also Grolier products.

Grolier's reference book publications are distributed in North America by a number of subsidiaries, including Grolier Interstate, Inc., Grolier Educational Corp., Scarecrow Press, Grolier Ltd. (Canada), Caribe Grolier (Puerto Rico), Lexicon Publications, Inc. (Grolier's wholesaling arm) and Franklin Watts, Inc.

In the international area, Grolier's reference book operations consist mainly of direct sales to consumers by commissioned representatives; the company's products include English and foreign-language multivolume encyclopedias, reference works and self-instructional courses in English and other languages.

In Latin America, Mexico continued to be Grolier's largest market, accounting for the major portion of sales and operating income in the area. Its 1980 sales increased by 29%, and its operating income by 17% over 1979 levels.

Grolier's direct mail marketing efforts include the sale of annual supplements and yearbooks to customers of its reference sets; the company has a proprietary mailing list of 3 million names for use in its direct mail marketing efforts.

After two decades of difficulties and a major crisis in the 1970s, Grolier appears to have finally developed a base from which to grow. Much of that growth is going to depend on the ability to develop new or updated products for the domestic home and library markets.

Grosset & Dunlap, Inc.
(a Filmways company)
51 Madison Ave.
New York, NY 10010
(212) 689-9200

The bulk of Grosset & Dunlap (G&D) library sales comes from its juvenile titles, which, in turn, generate a large portion of its total revenues. In addition to selling books to libraries, G&D library editions can be ordered with fully processed Library Journal Catalog Card kits, processed with Mylar jackets. These kits are produced by using Library of Congress MARC tapes, and processed books are shipped separately from Specialized Service and Supply Co., Cincinnati, OH.

Grosset & Dunlap has grown both internally and by acquisition, the latter including Ace Books (paperback) and Platt & Munk (juvenile books). Currently, about $18 million, or a little more than 50% of G&D's publishing revenues come from Ace's mass market paperbacks.

Among the titles which sell well in the library market are its series books, including the *Bobbsey Twins*, the *Hardy Boys* and *Nancy Drew*. Grosset & Dunlap publishes series for juvenile, middle grades and young adult/adult levels, offering 10% to 15% additional discounts to libraries on its most popular series books.

G&D has changed its method of marketing, no longer employing its own direct salesforce in the field. Telephone sales and direct mail are now stressed. The company has developed a 64-page catalog and uses it for direct mail solicitation twice a year.

About 7% of its juvenile sales are believed to be to the school and library market. The company does its own library bindings for many of these titles. Although its library sales have been hurt by poor funding patterns in school and public libraries, the company has been aggressive about marketing and discounting books for libraries, and the addition of the Platt & Munk line should also help sales of juvenile books.

The past couple of years have been unsettling for the company, with a loss of more than $8 million in operating income in fiscal 1980 and $6 million in fiscal 1981. The biggest drop in 1981 publishing revenues was caused by sale of the company's publishing distributing subsidiary in the fourth quarter of fiscal 1980. Grosset & Dunlap has been reported to be for sale for some time.

Harcourt Brace Jovanovich
757 Third Ave.
New York, NY 10017
(212) 888-4444

Harcourt Brace Jovanovich (HBJ) is a diversified company with interests in school publishing, which still generates 44.3% of its annual revenue; university and professional publishing; popular enterprises (via its 1977 acquisition of Sea World); periodical subscriptions and advertising; general books; tests and testing services; and insurance. Marvin Josephson Associates (MJA), which has interests in motion pictures and television, acquired 8.6% of HBJ in November 1978. HBJ responded to the MJA stock purchase by filing a complaint against that company. In 1978, the company pruned a number of troublesome operations, including Jove Publications, Inc., Guidance Associates, *Human Nature* magazine, and a radio broadcast investment.

In terms of activities in the library market, HBJ's Academic Press, together with its medical subsidiary, Grune & Stratton, and Johnson Reprint Corp., have been star performers. Academic Press, Sea World and the Harvest (insurance) companies are HBJ's three most profitable subsidiaries.

Academic Press has annual revenues of $50 million. It publishes scientific works in New York and, through its British subsidiary, in London. Its books and journals span a variety of scientific fields, including the natural, physical and behavioral sciences with emphasis on biochemistry, biology, mathematics, chemistry, psychology, physics, economics, archaeology and sociology. Academic Press publishes more than 600 new books and over 140 journals annually, many of the latter sponsored by scientific and learned societies. Sales of Academic's serial publications, major reference works and journals are largely to scientific, technical and medical libraries, while its treatises, monographs and journals are also sold to students and specialists in educational, industrial and research institutions.

Sales of the publications of the Academic Press group, including Grune & Stratton and Johnson Reprint Corp., are made via direct mail as well as by personal calls on booksellers, libraries and faculty members. Some 50% of Academic's sales come from outside the U.S. and the United Kingdom.

The Academic Press group has carved specialized niches for itself within the professional publishing field. Given HBJ's substantial marketing organization and its reliance on the Group's contribution to earnings, Academic's future within HBJ seems secure. And in view of the substantial worldwide market for technical and scientific publications, a market in which Academic is a dominant force, it should be well positioned to compete in that market in the 1980s.

Harper & Row
10 East 53 St.
New York, NY 10022
(212) 593-7000

Harper & Row is an old-line publishing company, with origins dating back to Harper & Brothers, founded in 1817. Harper & Row was organized in 1962 via the consolidation of Harper & Brothers and Row, Peterson & Co. It has grown substantially in the 1970s both internally and externally, the latter by acquisition of T.Y. Crowell in April 1977 and J.B. Lippincott in September 1978.

The Crowell acquisition gave Harper & Row additional strength in the trade, reference, college and juvenile markets while the Lippincott acquisition will aid Harper & Row in the trade, juvenile, religious, medical and educational publishing ends of its business.

Harper & Row's major institutional markets are school and college libraries for its school and college textbooks and public and school libraries for its trade books and children's books.

Approximately 60%-65% of children's book sales currently are to libraries versus approximately 80% in fiscal 1978; these sales exceeded $12 million in fiscal 1981 alone. Children's book revenues have been strong in the latter part of the 1970s and early 1980s, increasing 105.3% from fiscal 1977 to fiscal 1981.

Harper & Row and its subsidiaries publish 1200 titles each year, and its list includes many prestigious authors whose books libraries like to have on their shelves. The list includes Peter F. Drucker, Aleksandr I. Solzhenitsyn and Saul Bellow. In the juvenile area, Harper & Row's list is peppered with the likes of Maurice Sendak, Arnold Lobel and Katherine Paterson (who won a National Book Award in 1977 and the Newbery Medal in 1978 and 1981). It also publishes the *Little House on the Prairie* books.

Moore-Cottrell Subscription Services, Inc.
(subsidiary of Cadence Industries Corp.)
North Cohocton, NY 14868
(800) 828-6301

Moore-Cottrell, founded in 1869, has been a division of Cadence Industries, a magazine circulation company, since 1968. It has been providing periodical subscription service to libraries for over 100 years. It claims to provide six advantages to libraries utilizing its services: keeping them up to date with information on all domestic and foreign titles, ordering and prepaying individual subscriptions with each publisher, simplifying payment by issuing one annual consolidated invoice, processing all renewals and other changes, offering a special service for orders of five or fewer subscriptions and providing local trained sales representatives. Offerings include newspapers, consumer magazines, professional journals, monographs, annuals and standing orders.

Moore-Cottrell quotes on libraries' lists based on desired publications and subscriptions terms. Its prices are based on the margin granted by periodical publishers; handling charges are added when that margin is insufficient to meet its operating costs.

Moore-Cottrell has a computerized small order department that processes small orders (under five subscriptions) in under a week. It also offers a bibliographical service, a substitution service and foreign journal delivery. It publishes two catalogs annually, one for schools and public libraries and one for college, research, corporate and technical libraries. In addition, the company offers what it calls The Librarians's "Browser," a merchandising package of publishers' periodicals literature which it assembles. The "Browser" is an additional source of income for Moore-Cottrell, since it charges publishers $25 per thousand, with a minimum order of 5000 for inclusion. There is one "Browser" for publications aimed at schools and libraries, another for colleges, business, technical and research libraries.

Moore-Cottrell also publishes an annual *Librarians's Guide to Periodicals,* for academic, public, scientific and corporate librarians, and *The Condensed Guide to Periodicals for School and Public Libraries.* A quarterly newsletter, *Periodically Speaking,* provides information on company news, special subscription services and new periodicals.

OCLC (Online Computer Library Center)
6565 Frantz Rd.
Dublin, OH 43017
(614) 764-6000

OCLC (Online Computer Library Center), formerly The Ohio College Library Center, is a not-for-profit corporation organized to establish and operate a national, computerized network of bibliographic, cataloging services for libraries. It maintains eight large Sigma computers providing online access to a data base of more than 7.5 million bibliographic records.

Membership was originally restricted to libraries in Ohio, with libraries outside Ohio using its services by paying fees. However, as the result of a study done by Arthur D. Little, Inc., OCLC trustees voted in late 1977 to open the doors to board membership by creating a Users Council that elects six representatives to a 15-member board. The move was seen as another significant step in the evolution of OCLC into a national cataloging network. The opening up of board membership also provided a resolution to users' quest for self-determination: every OCLC user library is now a member of OCLC, Inc.

OCLC's history in the 1970s has been one of rapid growth, which, in turn, has allowed for a decrease in participants' costs for use of OCLC's online cataloging systems. OCLC provided 39.6 million catalog cards in 1976, 60.9 million in 1977, 82.4 million in 1978, 101.6 million in 1979 and 113.2 million in 1980. Billable first-time uses rose from 4.1 million to 10.5 million in that same period.

In spring 1981 OCLC announced it was making major changes in its price structure in the face of a changing library environment and a leveling off of online cataloging. OCLC increased the basic first-time use (FTU) charge from $1.36 to $1.40. At the same time, the prepayment discount was increased from 6% to 7% for those paying annually in advance; thus its FTU charge only rose from $1.27 to $1.30. (Currently OCLC's principal source of revenue, FTUs are projected to total 10.3 million during 1981-1982.) OCLC also instituted a monthly system service fee of $25 for each terminal on a dedicated leased telephone line and began to pass along postage costs to those ordering catalog cards.

OCLC, Inc. is the acknowledged leader among the computer utilities serving online users. It strength in number of users (over 2268), its assets (up from $13.6 million in fiscal 1977 to $57.9 million in fiscal 1980) and its emergence from being a local network to one that serves the entire United States position it well to remain the pre-eminent provider of online services in the 1980s.

Plenum Publishing Corp.
227 West 17th St.
New York, NY 10011
(212) 255-0713

Plenum was founded in 1946 by Earl M. Coleman, who retired as board chairman in July 1977. Its revenues come from journal subscriptions (40.9% in 1979) and books and tapes (46.7% in 1979 versus 48.2% in 1978). About 80% to 90% of Plenum's sales come from sales to libraries. The Plenum Press Division-Books publishes scientific, technical and medical books for use by professionals and their supporting libraries and other institutions. During 1980, Plenum Press published 272 new titles compared to 212 in 1976; it had an active backlist of some 2400 titles as of Dec. 31, 1980. The Plenum Press Division-Journals published 54 journals in 1980.

Plenum has a Consultants Bureau imprint which dates back to 1949 and publishes English translations of Russian scientific journals and special research reports. The Consultants Bureau has a contractual relationship wth VAAP, the Soviet Union copyright agency. The Consultants Bureau imprint currently publishes English translations of society journals. In 1980 it published nine Russian language books in English translation. Consultants Bureau also produces English translations of 12 Russian journals for publication under contract by scholarly societies.

Plenum's DaCapo Press subsidiary publishes reprints of scholarly works in musicology, jazz, architecture and decorative art, photography, graphic arts, history and literature.

IFI/Plenum Data produces the IFI Comprehensive Data Base of Patents, a computerized index file containing references to all U.S. chemical and chemically related patents issued since January 1950. J.S. Canner & Co., acquired by Plenum in 1968, is a major supplier of back-issue periodicals to university, college and industrial libraries throughout the world. Plenum Publishing Co. Ltd. (London) affords Plenum a marketing and editorial base in the U.K., Europe and Middle East.

Plenum has been able to achieve higher growth rates than many other

THE SHRINKING LIBRARY DOLLAR

publishers selling to the library market by entering new areas of publishing, such as text-reference books on the graduate and senior undergraduate levels in science and engineering, clinical medicine books for practicing physicians and medical students, and nonresearch-oriented books. However, because of its heavy dependence on the library market, Plenum will be affected more than many other publishers by negative trends in library funding.

Prentice-Hall, Inc.
Englewood Cliffs, NJ 07632
(201) 592-2000

Close to half of Prentice-Hall's sales are from textbooks and educational materials, primarily college textbooks (it is the leading publisher in that area), with most of the balance coming from business and professional and subscription products (26%) and business and other professional books (13%).

Prentice-Hall's general books marketing organization promotes and sells bound books drawn from the company's college, educational, professional and trade lists to booksellers as well as to public, school and special libraries. One-fourth of sales by this organization are to libraries, the balance to the retail trade. Library sales are direct as well as through wholesalers. In addition to selling its regular list to the library market, Prentice-Hall has a number of smaller companies to which library sales are important. These include Spectrum Books, publisher of instructional, informative books in both paper and cloth editions, and Reading Enrichment Co., Inc., which markets motivational reading programs to libraries as well as schools and other institutions.

A few years ago, Prentice-Hall acquired Arco, publisher of test preparation books for professional and civil service examinations. On December 11, 1979, the company acquired Deltak, Inc., the leading producer of multimedia training programs for high technology industries, including data processing and communications.

Prentice-Hall's looseleaf services division calls libraries an "appreciable" market for its services, with most library sales coming from law libraries and institutions funded by the federal, state and local governments. Its looseleaf services which sell well in the library market include *Federal Taxes Service, Federal Tax Guide* and *Executive Report*. Looseleaf services are sold on a subscription basis through mail and direct sales calls.

Unlike many major publishers, which depend heavily on juvenile book sales for healthy library market sales, Prentice-Hall's offerings to libraries are spread over a broader range. Because Prentice-Hall is not dependent on the types of libraries where funding is most depressed, it should do better than many other publishers in the 1980s in generating library market sales.

System Development Corp.
2500 Colorado Ave.
Santa Monica, CA 90406
(213) 820-4111

System Development Corp. (SDC) is a nationwide distributor of online computer-based bibliographic data services, competing with Dialog Information Services and Bibliographic Retrieval Services.

SDC, which derives the bulk of its revenues from federal government (mainly Defense Department) contracts, has provided access to the MEDLARS data base since 1969-1970 and to the ERIC (Educational Resources Information Center) data base since 1971 (both under the auspices of the Department of Health, Education and Welfare). At the end of the 1978, SDC's Search Service provided online access to three dozen data bases. Some of these were also accessed by Lockheed; others were exclusively with SDC. The latter include files on pollution, petroleum, life sciences, ecology, geosciences, telecommunications and the extensive material in its LIBCON file prepared by Information Dynamics Corp. The number of data bases, which are searched via a proprietary retrieval system called ORBIT, is constantly growing and totaled about 80 at the end of 1980.

The SDC Search Service has a different rate structure for each of the data bases it offers, but a single quantity discount plan applies to all the bases, based on hours billed per month. The volume discount increases incrementally with each hour of use and is computed against total connect hours billed on users' monthly invoices.

In addition to constantly increasing the number of data bases, SDC has lengthened service hours to global customers in different time zones.

In December 1980, the Search Service became available to Japanese subscribers from a Tokyo computer center managed by SDC Japan. In a move to tap the growing European online market, SDC and Derwent Publications Co. of London, England, have announced establishment of a European online information retrieval service as a joint venture.

THE SHRINKING LIBRARY DOLLAR

University Microfilms International
(a Xerox Publishing company)
300 North Zeeb Rd.
Ann Arbor, MI 48106
(313) 761-4700

University Microfilms International, founded in 1938, and sold to Xerox in 1962, does publishing by xerography and lithography as well as on roll microfilm and microfiche. There are three sectors to its business, each headed by a general manager. The largest sector is serials, the second largest is dissertations and the third is books and collections.

The bulk of University Microfilms' business is to libraries, with heaviest concentration in the research area. Customers include public, university research and special libraries.

The company's basic business is the preservation on film of the written word; to this end, it has some 1 million copies of new and old books, magazines, theses and newspapers stored on film. In addition to domestic publications, University Microfilms stores current copies of hundreds of national and international magazines and newspapers, to which many libraries and schools subscribe. At the end of 1978, the company had 12,000 periodicals alone on microform.

University Microfilms also makes abstracts of doctoral dissertations available through online services, and claims there has been an explosion of interest since it became known that such dissertations can be made available on microform in a short period of time.

Its products are marketed by a combination of direct sales and direct mail; at the end of 1980, the sales staff included 13 field sales reps and 14 in-house reps responsible for telephone sales.

John Wiley & Sons, Inc.
605 Third Ave.
New York, NY 10158
(212) 850-6000

Wiley claims to have approximately 4% of the market for U.S. published professional books (other than medical books) and approximately 1% of U.S. published medical books.

Wiley's Professional Group includes the Wiley-Interscience Division, which accounts for about two-thirds of the company's revenues from professional publishing, and has a list which includes books and journals on the graduate or research level in the natural and applied sciences and engineering. A major product of this division is the third edition of the Kirk-Othmer *Encyclopedia of Chemical Technology* which will eventually number 25 volumes.

Ronald Press, acquired in 1977, publishes advanced works in business, management, finance, economics and accounting, while Wiley Ltd. (Chichester, England) and Halsted Press also publish professional books. Other components of the Professional Group are Wiley Self-Teaching Guides, the Professional Development Program and the Domestic Marketing Department.

Wiley markets professional and reference works through trade bookstores, jobbers and libraries. It once estimated that 13% of its sales were to the library market, with marketing efforts to libraries concentrated on direct mail. However, the shrinking library market has caused Wiley to discontinue over 45 scientific and technical series in the past 10 years. Overall, direct mail campaigns reportedly produced more than 25% of all its professional nonadoption book sales in fiscal 1980.

In addition to the U.S. library market, Wiley, which had an estimated $26.7 million in international sales in fiscal 1980, has its own staff of sales representatives who visit educational institutions as well as bookstores and libraries in major foreign markets. The latter include Mexico, Central and South America, Spain, India, Canada and Australia. International sales now account for 34% of company revenue.

Growth in educational materials revenues, largely college textbook sales, outpaced growth in professional and reference materials and services between 1973 and 1977. Sales of educational materials accounted for 52.8% of Wiley revenue in fiscal 1980. However, Wiley has taken steps to augment its Professional Group. These include the acquistion of Ronald Press, which has a strong list in advanced business, management, finance and accounting titles, and the internal growth of the Wiley Medical Division, which concentrates on meeting continuing educational needs of physicians and nurses through textbooks, monographs, reference works and journals. In 1979, Wiley acquired the St. Clair Press, a college textbook publisher, and in 1980 it acquired Professional Publications, Inc., a Florida-based publisher of materials for CPA review courses. In January 1981, Houghton Mifflin sold its medical publishing division, Houghton Mifflin Professional Publishers, Inc., to Wiley for a price reportedly under $1 million. Medical Division sales more than quadrupled from 1975 to 1980.

THE SHRINKING LIBRARY DOLLAR

The H.W. Wilson Co.
950 University Ave.
Bronx, NY 10452
(212) 588-8400

H.W. Wilson, founded in 1898 by Halsey W. Wilson, is a privately owned company that publishes reference works for libraries in four categories: magazines, monographs, indexes and book catalogs. It is considered the world's largest publisher of indexes and reference works for libraries including the widely used *Reader's Guide to Periodical Literature.*

Wilson's yearly title output varies according to how many monographs are done; its other publications, except for an occasional additional index, remain constant. Twenty titles were published in 1977, 18 in 1978, 14 in 1979 and 12 in 1980.

Wilson runs its own presses and does its own distribution, and no changes in the type of publications it produces are anticipated. Change is coming in the type of printing done by Wilson, however: the company has moved from letterpress to offset, and says its printing will eventually be automated so that indexes will be available in other than print format.

Wilson charges customers for some of its discipline-oriented publications, on what it calls the service basis method, based on principle that each subscriber should pay in proportion to the amount of service used. Wilson determines rates based on two indexes; periodical indexes, for which subscription price is based on indexed periodicals to which a given library subscribes, and book indexes, including *Cumulative Book Index* and *Book Review Digest,* for which price is determined according to the library's book fund. Such orders must be placed directly with Wilson rather than through subscription order agencies. Wilson claims the service basis method of charge makes its publications available to libraries which could not afford flat rates. In addition, the method reduces the cost to larger institutions by allowing smaller libraries to subscribe and thus contribute a share toward initial cost of publication.

There is no relationship between H.W. Wilson Company and H. Wilson Corp. (South Holland, IL), a manufacturer of audiovisual library furniture and equipment.

Wilson, which employs some 600 people, established the H.W. Wilson Foundation in 1952 to donate money to endeavors which advance libraries and librarianship.

Selected References

Atherton, Pauline, and Christian, Roger W. *Libraries and Online Services*. White Plains, NY: Knowledge Industry Publications, Inc., 1977.

Bahr, Alice Harrison. *Automated Library Circulation Systems, 1979-80*. White Plains, NY: Knowledge Industry Publications, Inc., 1979.

————*Book Theft and Library Security Systems, 1981-82*. White Plains, NY: Knowledge Industry Publications, Inc., 1981.

————*Microforms: The Librarians' View, 1978-79*. White Plains, NY: Knowledge Industry Publications, Inc., 1978.

————*Video in Libraries: A Status Report, 1979-80*. White Plains, NY: Knowledge Industry Publications, Inc., 1980.

Boss, Richard. *Library Technology Reports*. Chicago, IL: American Library Association, January 1979.

The Bowker Annual of Library & Book Trade Information. New York: R.R. Bowker Co., 1980.

Christian, Roger. *The Electronic Library: Bibliographic Data Bases, 1978-79*. White Plains, NY: Knowledge Industry Publications, Inc., 1978.

Compaine, Benjamin M. *The Book Industry in Transition: An Economic Analysis of Book Distribution and Marketing*. White Plains, NY: Knowledge Industry Publications, Inc., 1978.

The Data Bases Market. New York: Frost & Sullivan, Inc., 1977.

Dessauer, John P.; Doebler, Paul D.; and Nordberg, E. Wayne. *Book Industry Trends 1977*. Research Report No. 4. Darien, CT: Book Industry Study Group Inc., 1977.

————*Book Industry Trends 1978*. Research Report No. 5. Darien, CT: Book Industry Study Group, Inc., 1978.

————*Book Industry Trends 1980*. Research Report No. 10. Darien, CT: Book Industry Study Group, 1980.

Fry, Bernard M., and White, Herbert S. *Publishers and Libraries: The Study of Scholarly and Research Journals.* Lexington, MA: D.C. Heath/Lexington Books, 1976.

Grant, Vance, and Lind, George C. *Digest of Education Statistics 1977-78.* Washington, DC: Department of Health, Education and Welfare, 1978.

Improving State Aid to Public Libraries. Washington, DC: National Commission on Libraries and Information Science, 1977.

Ladd, Boyd. *National Inventory of Library Needs-1975.* Washington, DC: National Commission on Libraries and Information Science, 1977.

Martin, Susan K. *Library Networks, 1981-82.* White Plains, NY: Knowledge Industry Publications, Inc., 1981.

National Commission on Libraries and Information Science. *Evaluation of the Effectiveness of Federal Funding of Public Libraries.* Washington, DC: Supt. of Documents, U.S. Government Printing Office, 1976.

Smith, Stanley V. *Library Statistics of Colleges and Universities, Fall 1975 Institutional Data.* Washington, DC: National Center for Education Statistics. U.S. Department of Health, Education and Welfare, 1977.

Statistics of Public Libraries, 1974 (LIBGIS I), Monograph No. 15, Urbana-Champaign, IL: University of Illinois Graduate School of Library Science, 1978.

Statistics of Public School Library Media Centers, 1978 (LIBGIS I). Monograph No. 14. Urbana-Champaign, IL: University of Illinois Graduate School of Library Science, 1978.

Whitestone, Patricia. *Photocopying in Libraries: The Librarians Speak* White Plains, NY: Knowledge Industry Publications, Inc., 1977.

Williams, Martha E., ed. *Annual Review of Information Science and Technology.* White Plains, NY: Knowledge Industry Publications, Inc., 1981.

Index

Abel, Richard, 58, 108
Academic libraries, 1, 9-11, 22-27, 46, 60, 62, 65, 70, 87, 105, 113, 119, 120, 128-129, 133
funding, 38-43
Academic Press, 66, 84
AMS Press, 67
American Institute of Physics, 82
American Library Association, 6, 10, 54, 93, 103, 114
Association of Research Libraries, 26, 87
Audiovisual market, materials, 5, 13, 15, 34, 111-118
Baker & Taylor, 53, 57, 59, 61, 69, 74, 107, 108, 113, 142-143
BALLOTS, 107
Banta, G., 58, 118,
Bell & Howell Micro Photo Division, 120, 121, 122, 123
Bender, Matthew, 68
Bibliographic Retrieval Services, 94, 143-144
Bindings (for books), 119
Blackwell North America, 58, 69, 74, 79, 108, 144-145
Blom, Benjamin, 66
Book Industry Study Group, 7, 13, 27, 34, 46, 62, 64, 111, 119, 127
Book Review Digest, 56
Books in Print, 56
Booksmith, Dist. Co., 58
Boss, Richard, 103
Bowker Annual of Library and Book Trade Information, 34
Bowker, R.R., 56, 147-148

Brodart, 53, 57, 58, 61, 69, 74, 108, 111, 118, 145-146
CAPCON, 93
Cataloging and processing services, 104-106
Catalog subscription agencies, 77, 79-80
Center for the Humanities, 114
Checkpoint, 103, 104
Chemical Bank Research Library, 10, 36
Cincinnati Electronics, 102
CL Systems, 100, 103, 148-150
Columbia University School of Library Service, 10
Commerce Clearing House, 67, 136
Copyright Clearance Center, 6, 85, 139
Copyright laws, 6
Council of Library Resources, 88
CRM Films, 114
Cumulative Book Index, 56
Dartnell, 67
Data bases, 94-99
DataPhase, 100
Demco, 59, 118
Doubleday, 57, 61, 116
Dow Jones-Bunker Ramo, 95
Education amendments of 1974, 116
Electronic security, 103-104, 105
Encyclopaedia Britannica, 71, 113
Engineering Societies Library, 10, 36
Faxon, 79, 152

Federal libraries, 36-38
Federal programs for libraries, 38-41, 42
Field Enterprises, 71
Films Inc., 113, 114
Fry, Bernard M., 82
Gaylord Bros., 100, 103, 104, 114, 118, 152-153
Greenwood Press, 67
Grolier, 71, 153-154
Grosset & Dunlap, 51, 108, 154-155
Guidance Associates, 114, 116
Harcourt Brace Jovanovich, 66, 114, 116, 155-156
Harper & Row, 69, 156-157
Hewlett Packard Co. Libraries, 36
Horn Book, 55
Huntting, H.R., 58-60
Information Handling Services, 120, 122
Innovated Systems, 102
Irwin, Richard D., 67
Josten's 58, 118
Katz, Bill, 82
Kennikat Press, 67
King Research, 88
Knogo, 103, 104
Kraus Reprint Co., 67
Lawyers Coop, 68
Lea & Febiger, 69
Learning Corp. of America, 114
Library acquisitions, 1980s, 126-127
Library budgets, 23, 127-131, 137
Library Bureau, 118
Library of Congress, 93, 105-106, 109
Library funding, 38-40

Library furniture and supplies, 118-119
Library Journal, 55
Library markets
 audiovisual, 5, 34, 111-117
 economic trends, 3-4, 140
 general books, 46-60, 135
 overview, 1, 9-43
 periodicals, 75-89, 139
 professional and reference, 62-74, 135-136
 systems, 92-109, 138-139
Library networks, 92-110
Lippincott, J.B., 69
Lockheed Information Systems, 95, 96, 124
Macmillan, 55, 57, 61, 66, 69, 71
Magazines, see periodicals
Magazines for Libraries, 77, 82
MARC, 93, 105-106, 108
McGraw-Hill, 67, 69, 72, 114
Mead Data Central, 95
Metropolitan Museum of Art Library, 10
Microform sales, 119-121
Micropublishing, 122-123
3M/Tattle Tape, 105
Moore-Cottrell Subscription Services, 79, 157-158
More, Thos. Assoc., 57
Mosby, C.V. 69
National Center for Education Statistics, 27
National Comm. on Libraries and Information Science, 41
National Inventory of Library Needs, 15, 17, 23, 27, 44, 115
National Library of Medicine, 96
National Microfilm Library, 123
National Periodicals Center, 88
NELINET, 93

Index

Nemeyer, Carol, 66
New York Times Information Bank, 96-97
1977 Directory of Special Libraries, 34
Oceana Publications, 68
OCLC, Inc., 93, 102, 105, 107, 137, 158-159
Online services, 94-99
Pergamon Press, 84, 121, 122
Periodicals, 75-90, 136
Plenum Publishing, 159-160
Plessey Corp. (England), 103
Prentice-Hall, 66, 67, 160-161
Proposition 6, 58
Public libraries, 9, 11-22, 46, 64, 113, 128, 132-133
  funding, 38-43
Publishing, professional and reference, 62-74, 135-136
  law books, 68
  medical books, 68-69
  scholarly reprints, 66-67
  subscription reference books, 71-72
Publishing, trade books
  adults, 48-49, 138
  distribution, 53-54
  juvenile, 49-51, 138
  mass market, 51-52
Publishing, university press books, 70-71
Purdue Univ. Mathematical Sciences Library, 10
Reader's Guide to Periodical Literature, 77, 81
Research Libraries Group, 88
Saunders, W.B., 69
School enrollments, 3
School libraries, 10, 27-34, 60, 64, 111, 129-130, 133-134
  funding, 38-43
School Library Journal, 55
Scribners, 57-61
Sentronic, 104
Society for Visual Education, 113
SOLINET, 93
Special libraries, 10, 34-36, 46, 60, 87, 113, 119, 120, 127, 130-131, 134
Special Libraries, 88
Special Libraries Association, 34, 88
System Development Corp., 96-98, 161
Systems Control Inc., 102
Thames Book Co., 57
Time-Life Films, 113, 114
Universal Library Systems Ltd., 102
University of Chicago Press, 84
University of Texas (Austin) Libraries, 23, 36
University Microfilms, 120, 121, 122, 162
Van Nostrand Reinhold, 66, 67, 72
Video In Libraries, A Status Report, 115
Washington & Lee Law School Library, 36
West Publishing, 68
Wiley, John, 66, 67, 69, 72, 162-163
Williams & Wilkins, 69, 136
Wilson, H.W. Co., 164
Xerox Electro-Optical Systems, 106
Xerox University Microfilms, *see* University Microfilms

About the Authors

Dantia Quirk is vice president and general manager of publishing periodicals, Knowledge Industry Publications, Inc. Previously she was managing editor of the *Educational Marketer* newsletter and subsequently served as editor of all five Knowledge Industry Publications newsletters. In addition, she is involved in the publication of daily newspapers at various conventions. After receiving her B.A. from Mount Holyoke college, Ms. Quirk worked at *Seventeen Magazine*, and later as managing editor of a group of newspapers owned by the *Independent Herald of Westchester*.

Ms. Quirk is the author of five publishing industry studies and is co-author of *Crisis! The Taxpayer Revolt and Your Kids' Schools*.

Patricia Whitestone is the author of *Photocopying in Libraries: The Librarians Speak* and co-author of *Crisis! The Taxpayer Revolt and Your Kids' Schools*. After earning a B.A. in English from Connecticut College, she was an associate editor of *Seventeen Magazine*. She later worked for an educational publisher and was a freelance writer on a variety of subjects. Formerly senior editor, library and information publishing periodicals for Knowledge Industry Publications, Inc., she has edited such newsletters as *Advanced Technology/Libraries, Information and Data Base Publishing Report* and *Education Funding Reports*.

Other Titles from Knowledge Industry Publications

The Book Industry in Transition: An Economic Study of Book Distribution and Marketing
by Benjamin M. Compaine
LC   78-7527   ISBN   0-914236-16-4 $24.95

U.S. Book Publishing Yearbook and Directory, 1981-82
edited by Judith S. Duke
LC   79-649219   ISBN   0-914236-99-7 $60.00

Decision Making for Library Management
by Michael R.W. Bommer and Ronald W. Chorba
LC   81-17160   ISBN   0-86729-001-3 $34.50
                        ISBN   0-86729-000-5   (pbk) $27.50

Marketing the Library
by Benedict A. Leerburger
LC   81-18132   ISBN   0-914236-89-X $24.50